D0034791

A Grip of Time

A GRIP OF TIME

When prison is your life

LAUREN KESSLER

RED ⚡ LIGHTNING BOOKS

This book is a publication of

RED LIGHTNING BOOKS
1320 East 10th Street
Bloomington, Indiana 47405 USA

redlightningbooks.com
© 2019 by Lauren Kessler

Manufactured in the United States of America

ISBN 978-1-68435-078-0 (hardback)
ISBN 978-0-68435-080-3 (ebook)

1 2 3 4 5 24 23 22 21 20 19

To
Don, Eric, James, Jann, Jimmie, Kaz, Lee, Michael,
Michael2, Sterling, Wil

and to
Steven

The dreams have died within our hearts,
Grown cold and hard with time.
And all the words we vowed to speak,
When life was young and dear,
Died in silence, for they were
Words no one wished to hear.

—Jack Catron
Oregon State Penitentiary inmate, 1917

Do time.
Don't let time do you.

—Common prison expression

Author's Note

THIS IS A WORK OF NONFICTION.

The people in this book are real people. All the men in the writing group wanted their real names to be used. I have not knowingly changed any facts or details about their lives. I have changed the names of two people to ensure privacy. I have chronicled the events, incidents, and conversations in this book as faithfully and honestly as I know how. Most I directly witnessed. Some were written about or told to me by the men in the group.

Any liberties I have taken are liberties not of fact but of interpretation. I saw this place, these people, and these events through my own eyes and filtered them, as all nonfiction writers do, through my own sensibilities. I mean to tell truths both factual and emotional.

A Grip of Time

One

"MOVE TO THE SIDE," HE SAID, JERKING HIS HEAD TO THE
right.

I obeyed. Obeying is what you do when a prison guard tells you to
do something.

I had set off the metal detector. The guard, big, fleshy, bored, hardly
looked at me. I wasn't a threat. I was barely an annoyance. Someone
holding up the line.

"Step out of the way," he said again.

I was moving too slowly, trying to wedge myself between the wall
and the guard without touching the guard. I looked at him, thought
about saying something. Didn't.

I was shoeless, beltless, and jewelry-free. My pockets were empty. I
didn't know why I had set off the alarm. And so I stood to the side, silent,
awaiting further instructions, looking over my shoulder at a scene that
was becoming familiar to me: the Greyhound bus–style visitors' waiting
room with its linoleum floors and its plastic chairs; the dozens of weary
young women crowding in, jostling for position, carrying their fitfully
sleeping babies, holding tight to their squirming toddlers.

Like me, they were waiting to be "processed." Like me, they were
waiting to begin the trek—simultaneously tedious and frightening—
through the metal detector, down a long, blank corridor, through heavy
metal gates that clanged behind you, stopping at a checkpoint where you
traded your driver's license for a clip-on prison ID card and placed your
hand through a slot to be stamped with UV-visible ink, then through
another set of clanging gates, down an even longer corridor, past a

1

second checkpoint (state your name, show your ID), through a third gate, and on to the heavily guarded control floor that sat at the heart of this maximum-security prison. Somewhere along the line, the women and children peeled off to the big, featureless visitors' room where they could sit and talk with their inmate husbands, baby daddies, brothers, fathers. I would continue, accompanied by an officer, thirty feet across the control floor to another gate and up a flight of concrete stairs to the activities floor to meet with my inmate writers. This afternoon would be the fourth meeting of the writers' group I was working hard to get established at Oregon State Penitentiary (OSP).

—∞—

The state's oldest prison, its only maximum-security facility, and the site of the state's death row, OSP is home to more than two thousand men, although "home" is not the word that comes to mind to anyone who lives—or visits—here. The prison sits, invisible behind a twenty-five-foot-high concrete perimeter wall, less than a mile and a half from the pretty, golden-domed Oregon State Capitol building in the heart of sleepy Salem. Inside the walls is a twenty-two-acre self-contained city with the state's second-largest commercial laundry, a furniture factory, a metal fabrication shop, a call center, vocational and hobby shops, an infirmary, two recreation yards—and four cell blocks, three of them massive Sing Sing–style cages within cages that look like the setting of every grim prison movie ever made: parallel rows of barred cells, forty cells long, five tiers high, narrow metal walkways, nothing but concrete and steel.

The drive into the prison grounds is as lovely as the prison is not. This is fertile Willamette Valley river bottom land. The penitentiary entrance is landscaped and manicured. There are brilliant-green lawns and towering conifers, graceful weeping willows and stately oaks. There are rosebushes and hydrangeas. There are birds. And then there aren't. Up the set of concrete steps and into the main building, a late-nineteenth-century edifice that looks like a cross between an asylum and an aged urban high school in a not-great neighborhood, there is the tired waiting room with vending machines and an old ATM and a long counter for processing visitors and a TSA-style conveyor belt and metal detector overseen by guards like the one who had just pulled me aside.

—⁓—

I stood, still waiting. I was not a veteran visitor like most of the worried and weary women queuing up at the counter, but I knew the drill: show picture ID at the counter, sign in, check pockets, stash purse in one of the twenty-five-cent lockers, stand in line, take off shoes, wait your turn to go through. I knew how to dress: Show as little skin as possible. Wear clothing that was loose enough not to be formfitting but not so loose as to look as if you were maybe trying to conceal something. Don't look too feminine. But don't look butch either. No jeans. The inmates wore jeans. Nothing blue. The inmates all dressed in blue. I had learned the rules, and I followed the rules. Months later, when I was steeping myself in research about prisons, I came across this chilling sentence by sociologist Megan Comfort: "Correctional officers . . . attempt to transform prison visitors into an obedient corps of unindividuated, nonthreatening entities that can be organized according to prison rules." That pretty much summed up the experience.

The guard ordered me to check my pockets (nothing), remove any jewelry (already done), and go through again. Again, the alarm sounded. I assumed that his next step was to call over a female guard to pat me down. Or he could take me aside and wand me, like the TSA guys do. A hassle, but either way I'd be good to go.

I was getting antsy. My writers' group was waiting for me upstairs on the activities floor: six guys, all members of the Lifers' Club, all convicted murderers. They were decades into their grip of time, serving either life with (the "with" being a possibility of parole) or life without (meaning they would die in prison). I had started working with them almost six months ago, coming in to run this writers' workshop I created. It was more of a struggle to make it happen than I had bargained for, and it was happening in fits and starts. One month I had permission to come in, the next, nothing. I was a volunteer-without-portfolio, so to speak. Unlike most of the nonfamily civilians who gained entrance to the prison, I was not part of a faith group or ministry, a veterans' organization, or a twelve-step recovery program. I was not sanctioned by the community college that had a contract to teach GED classes and run a small associate arts degree program or the university that taught a smattering of classes through a national program called Inside Out. I was just a writer looking to work with people who wanted to write. I saw writing as a way to give voice to the voiceless, which those behind bars certainly were. I saw writing as not merely self-expression but as deep, self-administered therapy, a way to process and learn from experience, a way to understand and make sense of a life that needed making sense of. That would be everyone's life, of course, but I was thinking about the kind of lives that got people into prison and the lives, the very long lives, those people lived once they got there.

And I was thinking about not only the people who lived those lives but also the rest of us, the ones who made the laws and paid the taxes to support the criminal justice and corrections systems, the ones who sat on juries that sentenced people to places like the one I was waiting to be processed into. I was thinking about how ignorant I, all of us, were about what happened inside these places. We thought we knew much more than we did. We had maybe read puff pieces about Martha Stewart's cushy five months at a facility that looked more like a private college than a prison. We had maybe read snarky features about Bernie Madoff strutting through the yard surrounded by groupies at Butner, the "crown jewel" of the federal prison system. And occasionally we heard news about a riot. Then, every few years, an exposé would surface about sweltering cells in southern prisons or cruel and ill-trained prison guards. Meanwhile we remembered scenes from *Shawshank Redemption* or binge-watched *Orange Is the New Black* and we figured we knew what was what. But of course we didn't.

Our ignorance, I was coming to think, was actually purposeful and, in odd ways, strategic. On the one hand, the prison system itself had a vested interest in keeping the world behind bars hidden from us. Our ignorance meant we were less likely to interfere with operations, to suggest new policies, to scrutinize budgets, to make a fuss. It made running the system easier and more efficient for those who ran the system. Of course, it also served to hide everything from outright abuses to casual cruelties to daily boredom. And it was so easy to do. All it took was tight control of the flow of information by communications and public relations staff and creating barriers to media access. On the other hand, the prison-as-hidden-world worked for those of us on the outside too. The murkier and more unknowable that world was, the easier it was for us not to care, the easier it was for us to feel no connection to the people inside. What did this alien netherworld have to do with us anyway? Maybe a lot. Maybe more than we wanted to consider.

And so the other reason I was here at OSP, why I wanted to help and encourage these men to write about their lives, was so that I could learn about this hidden world. So that we all could. I could teach these men how to craft stories. They could educate me about prison life. I needed to know—I thought we all needed to know—who these people were that we put away, far away from us, for life, in a country that puts more people in prison than any other country on earth. We needed to know what "life" meant when that life was spent almost entirely behind bars.

—⁂—

I stood there, waiting, eager to get upstairs and start the afternoon workshop. But today the guard wasn't going to let it happen. Maybe he didn't like the way I looked. Maybe he was having a bad day. I don't know. What I know is he made a spur-of-the-moment choice not to call a female officer to pat me down and not to wand me. He wasn't going to make it possible for me to get through the control point. I was frustrated, I was furious—and I was powerless. And I couldn't let it show. This same guard might be manning the metal detector on my next visit. I didn't want to make an enemy.

And then, all of a sudden, I got it. I got a whiff of what it was like to live inside these walls. Walking back to the locker to retrieve my stuff, I felt almost queasy with impotence. And I felt a little crazy, that kind of crazy you feel when things that made sense all of a sudden don't. I was in a place that was all about rules, that was dictated and constrained by rules. If you knew the rules and played by them, everything was predictable, and you were okay, right?

Wrong. Because prison was also a place of random acts. Knowing and obeying the rules didn't spare you from the random acts. The rules created the expectation of predictability. On the other hand, anything could happen. You were buffeted coming and going. And you never knew when it was going to happen. And you couldn't do a thing about it.

—∿—

It would be more than a month before I could meet with the guys again.

Two

I AM STANDING IN FRONT OF A ROOM FULL OF CONVICTS.
These men, fifty or sixty of them sprawled on metal folding chairs set up
in rows, have spent twenty, thirty, I don't know how many more years
in prison. A rivulet of sweat is snaking down the back of one of my legs,
inching its way to the heel of my shoe. While one part of my brain is
focused on what I am saying—a pitch for the writers' group I've been trying to get off the ground—another part of my brain is busy imagining the
headline in tomorrow's paper: "Inmates Hold Woman Writer Hostage at
State Pen." I tell myself that it is natural to feel fear. I am in a maximum-
security penitentiary. I am the only female in the room. The men in the
room have all done bad things, very bad things. On the other hand, there
are guards here. And, I remind myself, this is not a roomful of convicts
likely to jump me. It is a roomful of mostly balding, gray-bearded older
men who gather every other month for an officially sanctioned Seniors'
Day. It is a long-standing and long-popular event primarily, I am told,
because of the donuts—or, as displayed this afternoon on big tables at
the back of the room, the oversized, greasy apple fritters sitting on torn
sheets of brown paper towels.

I stare out into the big, high-ceilinged space that would look like an
all-purpose room in a seriously run-down middle school if it were not
for the wire cages that line the perimeter. Each little cage, the size of a
prison cell, bears the name of a different prison club: Uhuru, Lakato,
Veterans, NA/AA, Music, Asian Pacific Family, Lifers. It's the Lifers'
Club members I'm interested in, those men sentenced to spend most
if not all of their adulthoods here in prison. It's the lifers I want in my

7

writing group. They know the most about what it is like to live here, and I think they have the most important stories to tell. They also might be the most receptive to a new activity. Chances are, with decades behind bars, they've long exhausted the existing opportunities the prison offers. Many lifers, by virtue of their long periods of incarceration, are now seniors sitting here eating apple fritters.

"Senior" doesn't mean the same thing in prison as it does in the outside world, where the standard retirement age of sixty-five seems to be the demarcation. In prison, where research suggests that people age up to fifteen years faster than their nonincarcerated peers, a senior could be as young as forty-five. Many states count as "elderly" all prisoners older than fifty. At OSP more than 20 percent of the inmates are older than fifty-five. The oldest man in here is eighty-four. In the chairs facing me, I see men who look old enough to be my father but are probably the age of my younger brother. I see men who look like grizzled Hells Angels and men who look like trouble and men who look like kindly uncles and everyday middle-aged men—white, black, brown—who you would take no notice of on the street. They all wear blue denim jeans and dark-blue T-shirts stamped with the OSP logo.

I don't know if anyone is listening, but I am inviting them to be part of, or at least come just this once to, the group I'll be convening in a few minutes in a room down the hall from the fritter-laden table. I made this same pitch—find your voice, write what you know, write to make sense of it all—two months ago at a meeting of a select group of prisoners, staff, and outside educators dedicated to expanding learning opportunities inside. This was after I had spent close to six months trying unsuccessfully to persuade the local community college that offered basic education classes at the prison to sponsor my writing group—not hire me, not pay me, just make the group legit. I had no idea it would be this hard to volunteer my services.

The presentation to the advisory group had gone reasonably well. I had talked passionately about the power of telling your own story. I had fielded questions from a couple of inmates in the group who seemed genuinely interested. There was a tall, dreadlocked guy who introduced himself as Dez and said he was a writer. He was looking for opportunities to practice, learn, get better. He was a lifer, only forty but with more than twenty years behind bars, who was working on an autobiography. There was a sharp-tongued, steely-eyed man in his late seventies, also a lifer, who stared me down and challenged everything I said, but then seemed satisfied with my responses and said he might consider joining such a group if it came to be. The advisory group handed off my proposal to the Lifers' Club to see what could be worked out. The upshot was this invitation to pitch at Seniors' Day. I would piggyback our first session on this afternoon's event.

The men in this room, the seniors, most of whom are lifers as well, are a speck on the tip of the tip of the iceberg. The iceberg is the 2.3 million Americans behind bars, one out of nine of whom are serving life sentences, more than 30 percent of whom are forty-five or older. In fact, those older than fifty are the fastest-growing segment of the prison population, the numbers doubling every decade since 1990. In the months and months it had taken to get to the point of making my Seniors' Day pitch, I had been busy backgrounding myself on the historically unprecedented and internationally unique epidemic of US mass incarceration. I had discovered that the United States led the world in both number of people in prison and in the rate of incarceration. (Our rate is 716 per 100,000. For comparisons: Germany's is 76 per 100,000; Saudi Arabia's is 161; Russia's is 455.) We account for about 5 percent of the world's population and close to 25 percent of the world's prison inmates. From the 1980s—when tough-on-crime policies led to longer (mandatory) sentences and fewer paroles granted—the prison population had increased by 371 percent, while the US population had grown 37 percent. There are now four times as many lifers behind bars than there were in 1984. Fifty or sixty of them are sitting in front of me, maybe listening, as they quietly consume apple fritters and drink bad coffee from Styrofoam cups. How many would follow me into one of the rooms down the hall to join the first session of the writers' group?

The answer: three.

We sit on metal folding chairs in a small circle in an otherwise bare, echoey room that looks like the setting for an early Cohen brothers movie. I am now doubly nervous: first because it is the initial meeting, second because so few men show up. Make that triply nervous: I am, after all, convening a class of convicts. And not just convicts, lifers. You don't get life for shoplifting. You get life for doing something terrible. And yet, here they are, three of them, greeting me politely, hesitantly shaking my hand, sitting patiently in their prison blues, waiting to hear what I have to say. One man, slender, clean-cut, balding, maybe midfifties, is wearing fashionable eyewear and somehow manages to look put together, almost professional, in his prison uniform. He has an open face and a ready smile. Next to him sits a big, strapping, sixtyish guy with a blond-turning-to-gray handlebar moustache. He is still handsome in a fleshy way, and I can tell from the get-go that he is a man accustomed to using his charm. The third guy is sandy haired with a deeply lined and weathered tough-guy face. I mean a *tough-guy* face, a central casting thug face. I would cross the street to avoid him, and here he is five feet from me.

When I ask them to introduce themselves, I tell them that I don't want to know what they did to get in here, and I don't want to know their last names. If they tell me their full names, I know I will look them up in the system and learn more than I want to know right now. I don't want to know who they were decades ago, the men who committed the murder, the rape, the I-don't-know-what, the men capable of such acts. I want to, at least at first, see them for who they are today. I want to be able to listen, talk, read their work without seeing everything through the lens of their rap sheets. That sounds as if it comes from a more enlightened place than it does. The fact is, I need to stay ignorant to keep my fear at a manageable level. And I need to stay ignorant so that my judgmental self will not obstruct my ability to connect with them as writers, as people.

And so: Don, the fashionable one; Jann, the charmer; Red, the tough guy. They are all lifers. They are all seniors. They have all been inside for more than thirty years. That's all I know right now. I tell them I will teach them how to craft stories about their lives if they will teach me what it is like to live the lives they do. I tell them that I think writing is both a way of connecting with others and a way of understanding and making sense of yourself, that writing is hard and takes practice, that it can be both painful and joyful—and is almost always therapeutic. Because writers are always readers, I ask them what they've been reading. Don has taken many college classes and has read his share of literature and philosophy. Red is, it seems, a veteran of every self-help program the prison offers and knows that genre. He is also a committed Bible reader. Jann says he reads a lot but has trouble remembering the last book he's read. Almost a year ago, when I was a one-time guest in a community college class offered at OSP, I had a chance to peruse the prison library. It was clear from reading the titles of the few hundred books on the shelves that the major donors were faith-based groups and twelve-step programs. I wonder how I can teach them about writing if they don't have great writing to read and learn from.

We begin to work out a plan for the group. They say they know other guys who are interested but who couldn't come today. I urge them to spread the word. But I'm not exactly sure what word should be spread. Right now, we have no regular meeting time. I've been told that I can piggyback my writing group on the scheduled Seniors' Days, but those happen only four times a year. Three months between group meetings is a very long time. In between those times, I'm not sure how I can keep some semblance of activity alive. I don't know how I will get whatever they write or give them my feedback. They have no internet access, no email—in fact, no access to a computer to type a story. But I have worked too long to get to this point to let these challenges overwhelm the enterprise. And the men seem motivated.

I give them "homework." It is not so much a writing assignment as it is an observation and recording assignment. When life is monotonous, when it is lived in the same compound, following the same schedule, eating at the same time in the same place for years, for decades, it makes sense that you stop noticing. But a writer has to notice. A story lives through detail. I have to get them to notice again. The assignment is "A Week in the Life of [Don, Jann, Red]." You don't have to construct beautiful sentences, I tell them. Just talk to me on paper, I tell them. Just tell me about your routine. They seem both mystified that I would care and eager to tell me.

The logistics, which I work out during the next few weeks, are complicated. The men will give their writing homework to the inmate president of the Lifers' Club. He will then hand it off to a university professor who comes in once a week to teach a class. The professor will take the work back with him and leave it in his university mailbox. Then I'll drive to the university to pick up the work. My comments and feedback will be returned in the reverse order. There is nothing ideal about this situation, but it is what it is. Although my experience with the system is limited, I am already beginning to learn some of its lessons: You have to fight for every inch and consider it a victory when you get a millimeter. You can't make things happen. Other people control when and if things happen. In the meantime, I decide to ignore the "you can't make things happen" lesson—a lesson that, in truth, I hope never to take to heart—and continue to explore ways to set up regular meetings for the writing group.

A month later, I pick up an envelope at the university. In it are four "A Week in the Life" pieces, one from Red, one from Jann, one from Don, and one from someone named John who was not at the initial meeting. He must be one of the men the others said was interested but who couldn't come to our Seniors' Day session. Red's submission is twelve pages handwritten on lined notebook paper. This guy who looks like someone you wouldn't want to meet in a dark alley writes in exquisite script, the kind of careful cursive kids used to learn when penmanship was a subject and Ike was in the White House.

He begins: "I am 57 years old. Except for six months in 1985, I have been incarcerated since the 1980s."

The deadpan delivery gets to me. These simple, declarative sentences, so powerful, so packed, contain an entire life within them.

Red's week, if you read it as listings in someone's day planner, is completely ordinary: He wakes up early, has breakfast, goes to work, has lunch, goes back to work, has dinner, goes to sleep. In between times he reads or listens to music on the radio, talks to friends, visits with his wife. But interwoven with those mundane details are references to depression, the mental exhaustion he battles as he drags himself out of bed in the morning, the naps he takes every day not out of tiredness but to escape, the effort it takes to rally his spirits enough just to open his Bible, to persuade himself to go out to the yard for a breath of air, the effort he expends bottling up his anxiety when his wife visits because "she has enough trials of her own." Also almost on every page are references to his fear—his dread—about a task he must accomplish in the next few weeks: writing a personal statement for the parole board. Apparently he has secured a hearing with the board that could possibly result in a release date after more than thirty years inside. Every day he tries to write something or he agonizes over his inability to write something.

He visits the prison library to do research. He looks over the material he's collected that shows, he hopes, that he is a different person from the one who committed whatever crime or crimes got him here. He fears he doesn't know what to say, how to persuade them. The stress, he writes, "loops around my head." The possibility of freedom exhausts him; the reality that so few make parole threatens to rob him of hope. He crawls back into his bunk. He takes a nap.

Something else is interwoven in his days: fear for his health. He had a heart attack. He has a pacemaker. A prison doctor told him three years ago that a main artery in his heart is 90 percent blocked. At fifty-seven he feels—and in many ways is—old.

"I used to be able to handle myself," he writes.

Now, anxious for his own safety, fearful of becoming so incapacitated that he is sent to the prison's infirmary and never gets out, he is hyperalert to the challenges of growing old in this "violent environment." His view of his life is unsparing. His "Week in the Life" chronicle, its simple, unsentimental statements written in A-plus cursive, is painful to read. Yet he doesn't appear to feel sorry for himself. He knows he made this life he is living.

What stays with me, days after I have read and written comments on Red's homework, is this from the bottom of page 1: "I carry around an undercurrent of weariness. This life of constant routine has worn grooves in my soul."

This from the tough guy.

Don submits a nine-page chronicle of his week written in back-slanted, left-leaning penmanship so unusual that I look up its meaning on graphology websites. Apparently, despite generating great interest and enthusiasm throughout the twentieth century (not to mention being included in numerous TV police procedurals), graphology has proven to be a pseudoscience, which is a nice way of saying it's bullshit. Yet when I read the analysis of Don's severely slanted penmanship—"the writer has a defensive attitude . . . and represses impulses and need for affection and contact"—it's hard not to see this as potential insight into this quiet, self-contained man who has been behind bars for more than three decades.

Don writes about working swing shift in the towel section of the prison's immense commercial laundry, which he calls "the cotton fields."

It is tedious manual labor. He doesn't say how much he gets paid, but according to data gathered by the Prison Policy Initiative, it is less than fifty cents an hour. I wonder, when Don references "the cotton fields," if he knows about the critique of prisons as modern-day slave plantations.

When he isn't writing about sorting, washing, drying, and folding towels and rags, he writes about food: waffles for breakfast (he folds two into a paper towel and slides the packet into his jacket pocket for a snack later), a hastily made pancake and peanut butter sandwich (a gift for a friend on his sixty-ninth birthday), tomato soup, sloppy joes, ham au gratin, turkey noodle casserole, a fried egg sandwich, his disappointment over missing breakfast for every-other-Saturday cinnamon rolls. "Our time revolves around food and meals," he writes, noting that one of his favorite forms of entertainment on the outside was going out to eat at restaurants.

Unlike tough-guy Red, Don—giving credence to his graphological personality traits—offers little insight into how he feels about the life he lives. The routine, it seems, keeps him moving forward, step by step, folded towel by folded towel, meal by meal, blunting him, perhaps protecting him, from an inner life. Or maybe I am reading too much into this. Perhaps he is just not ready to share his inner life with a stranger.

Jann's piece is much shorter, two *typed* pages. Because (as I discover reading his week's chronicle) he volunteers to do paperwork and typing for the Lifers' Club, he has access to a word processor. His days, like those of all of the men here, are governed by the sleep-eat-work-eat-sleep prison schedule, controlled by the thirty-two bells that define their activities and movements. Like Red, he is concerned about his health. He is sixty-three. He writes that he quit smoking a year before tobacco was banned in the prison and managed to gain sixty-five pounds in his first few cigarette-free months. It took him a long time to get back to a manageable weight, but now he's there. He does some form of exercise every day. He watches what he eats and criticizes the prison chow for its high-starch/low-protein offerings. Like Red, he worries about becoming ill and getting a one-way ticket to the prison's infirmary. He worries about the expense of health care, writing that he has to pay $45.00 for an eye exam and $80.00 for a new pair of glasses—yet he makes an average of $51.00 a month at his prison job, a rate that he says has been the same since the 1990s. Back then, he writes, a bag of coffee from the prison canteen cost $5.00. Now it is $9.53. Every morning Jann makes himself a cup of coffee in his cell, using "fairly hot" tap water.

Unlike Red, whose wife visits him three times a week, Jann writes that he has no contact with family, no visits, no phone calls, no mail. "I am understandably a disgrace to them," he writes. "I am a convicted murderer and they have turned their backs on me." He's not looking for sympathy. He believes he deserves their scorn. And so he works, he volunteers, he hits the track for a brisk walk, he takes his allotted three showers a week, he watches a little TV. "It's like going through life on cruise control," he writes at the end of his week's chronicle. "I went to sleep one night a man of thirty-one and woke up one morning and looked into the face of a sixty-three-year-old man."

I learn a little bit about the daily routines of the mystery man, John, the guy who submitted work but didn't come to the Seniors' Day writers' group. I learn that he is fifty-four, that he arises at five and is asleep by eight thirty, that he, like Don, works in the prison's commercial laundry. He never misses breakfast because it's the only meal where milk is served. He watches a lot of NASCAR on the weekends. He's taking a college class and reading Tolstoy. Like Don's, his chronicle is informative but offers little insight into his state of mind, his temperament, his personality. It's actually what I expected when I assigned this first bit of homework. I wasn't prepared for the honesty and transparency I got from Red and Jann. Of course they revealed just what they chose to reveal, but the fact that they revealed *anything* about their emotional lives to a stranger, an outsider, is remarkable. I would like to think that this has something to do with the way I present myself. But I think it may have more to do with their hunger to be heard, to be listened to, by anyone.

—⁂—

One month has stretched into two, then three, with no resolution about regular meeting times for the group. Writing assignments are shuttling back and forth via our clunky system, which works about 50 percent of the time. I send back my comments, and based on what I read—a hint of a story, the mention of a character, a snippet of a conversation—I suggest new homework for each man individually. I have also made one group assignment, presenting as many choices as I can for them to stay engaged. Meanwhile Trevor, the Lifers' Club president, is seeing what he can do to schedule me into the club's meeting times (these are once a month) in addition to the four-times-a-year Seniors' Days.

Trevor is a go-getter: organized, energetic, and so professional in demeanor and conversation that it is hard to think of him as a convict or imagine him as a murderer. His relentlessly can-do attitude in a relentlessly can't-do environment is a testimony to some inner resolve, some deep aquifer of optimism that is almost beyond my understanding. Most of the lifers are a good twenty years older than Trevor and qualify to attend Seniors' Day, but he commands their respect. He has learned how to navigate the prison system with intelligence and a combination of skill, patience, and creativity that would make him a success in the world beyond these walls. If he ever gets out. Apparently, he has a chance.

As Trevor does his thing, I do mine, sending back an assignment that could open the door to storytelling without asking for full-blown stories. I don't want to ask for too much, and I would love to be able to *teach* some of the basics of narrative writing before I ask for it. The assignment is presented as a series of fill-in-the-blanks:

The last time I felt really happy was . . .
The last time I felt really sad was . . .
I feel most hopeful when . . .
I feel most hopeless when . . .
The last time I was very angry was . . .
The last time I honestly and joyfully laughed was . . .
The last time I cried was . . .
The most meaningful thing I did this week was . . .

I worry that these queries are too invasive. But I also know I am dealing with people who know how to protect their vulnerabilities better than most of us. It is how you stay alive, and sane, in prison. If someone does not want to respond, he won't.

When I pick up the envelope from the university, it's a little thicker than the last time. Inside I find work from Red (who is now signing his work as Jimmie), mystery-man John, Don, Jann, and a new man named Eric. The group is growing, up from three to five now, without us meeting again. I am encouraged. Don and Jann have chosen to write lengthy descriptions of their cells (one of the individual prompts I gave them). The other three, plus Don, responded to the fill-in-the-blanks assignment. I read them right then, sitting in the car in the university parking lot, because I can't wait until I get home. This writing provides a window into a hidden world. I want to look through that window.

Don literally invites me in. "Welcome to my world" is how he begins. He describes a cell he likens to a closet, a six-by-ten space that is so familiar to him he is astonished to read his own description of it. He hasn't noticed the details for so very long: white walls, gray floors, two bunks attached to the wall, sink, toilet, a small writing desk made from two shelves, a little window. From the little window, he can see out over the prison wall and all the way in the distance to Interstate 5, where he can barely make out the movement of cars and trucks. It's the best thing about the cell. He has lived here for thirty years.

Jann's cell is smaller, only five and a half by seven feet, although he dubs it "my palatial mansion here in Salem's finest resort." His bed measures six feet, three inches, but Jann is six foot four. A light fixture with a metal shade hangs from the seven-foot ceiling and hits him chin height. Noise is amplified along the cell block. He says it is like living inside a bass drum. He has a single cell on the top floor. He rejoices that he doesn't have a cellmate, a "cellie." He is happy for his vintage thirteen-inch TV, which he has kept in running order for decades. He mentions in passing that there is no heat in the top-floor cells except in the summer, when the heat rises from the tiers below and the hundreds of men who live there. He says that's when the temperatures often exceed one hundred degrees. I've seen pictures of the cells, at OSP and at other institutions. They are only a Google Images click away. But the lived experience, that is what comes through with their words.

As to the delicate, potentially emotionally invasive questions I asked in the fill-in-the-blanks assignment, Jimmie (Red), John, Don, and Eric have answered every one. I read through the pages slowly and carefully, imagining the backstories, the subtext, the scenes hinted at but not described. It is clear from their responses that the happiest moments are interactions with those on the outside. For Jimmie, it was marrying his wife in the prison visiting room in 2004, a story that I must get him to tell. For the new man I have yet to meet, Eric, it was hearing good news from the girlfriend who, he hopes, is waiting for him. She is an ex-con. After three years, she finally got a good job. John doesn't mention who he visited with, but he writes that the last time he was happy was ten days ago when he had a visitor. I read in the "last time I felt really sad" responses that John's mother died (and, of course, he wasn't with her) and that Eric recently found out that his son got a DUI and is addicted to painkillers.

Life goes on outside whether these men are there to experience it or not. They are hopeful for the same reasons we all are hopeful: when those around us are optimistic, when we get support, encouragement, and love. They despair over parole denials, legal setbacks, the inability to help those they love, the state of the world as it filters through televised evening news.

I am most interested to read their responses to the final prompt, the one that asks about the most meaningful thing they did this past week. The "Week in the Life of..." chronicles I read last month made clear the numbing sameness of their lives, the autopilot response to following the same schedule in the same place with the same people for decades. Is it possible to find meaning in a place that seems purposely designed to suck the meaning out of life? Eric finds meaning in a phone call with his son who is in the early days of drug rehab. Eric has been there, done that. At this late date, he is hoping he can be the father he never was. He looks for and finds meaning in working on this frayed connection. For Jimmie, the most meaningful event was his parole hearing, the one he was prepping for, stressing over, worrying about when he wrote his week's chronicle a few months ago. The hearing recently took place. He won't hear the news for perhaps more than a month. And so he waits.

I am still sitting in the car in the university parking lot. The parking meter has long expired. The meter reader has been by twice, staring at me through my windshield before moving on. I have one more "meaningful thing" item to read, Don's. I tear up when I read his response: "Writing with Lauren."

Three

ERIC HAS OFFICIALLY, IN PERSON, JOINED THE GROUP. He arrives at what is our third face-to-face session, a haggard and worried-looking man, deep furrows etched in his clean-shaven, prison-pale face. He has a thick head of reddish-brown hair. The face looks seventy. The hair looks thirty-five. Eric is in his late fifties. A few months ago, he got a date, meaning he was granted parole and was given a release date. It's almost two and a half years away, but when you've been in prison for most of your adult life—Eric has served three separate sentences, the last, this one, a two-decades-plus stretch—twenty-eight months doesn't seem like such a long time.

"I need the group," he says by way of introduction, not quite looking me in the eye. I wait for him to tell me why. "I need to keep my focus. Keep my head on straight," he says. That's when he tells me about his release date. He delivers what I would think would be extraordinarily good news as if he were instead informing me of the date of his execution. I congratulate him, shake his hand again.

"You don't seem particularly happy about this," I venture, not wanting to ask a direct question.

"Yeah," he says, looking down, "well, I've been through this before." Long pause. "Twice."

I nod.

"I need this time to be different," he says. "I need to remind myself, in writing, how this time is going to be different. I need to remind myself of all the reasons I have to stay clean this time."

In the last piece Eric submitted, which made its way to me ever so slowly through our clunky conduit, he wrote about "the most important decisions I make." I had prompted him to write about decisions based on something he mentioned in a previous piece about struggling to maintain a sense of personal control in prison. In this new piece, handwritten in pencil on three-hole loose-leaf paper like schoolboy's work, he focused on his decision to stay "clean, sober and crime free." In three pages he detailed the downward trajectory of his past, from a hardworking family man and father of two who enjoyed drinking and sometimes getting high, to an alcoholic and meth addict, to an addict who sold drugs to support his habit, to a meth manufacturer, to, finally, a guy who found himself behind the wheel of a car one December night in 1996, involved in a high-speed chase with police. He couldn't stop. He had drug-manufacturing chemicals in the car, and he'd already been in prison twice on drug charges. He didn't detail how it happened exactly, but he crashed into an automobile driven by a sixty-eight-year-old woman—he refers to her by name, Mrs. Amerson—who was on her way to go Christmas shopping. She died. A three-time loser, he went to prison for twenty-five to life.

I didn't want any of the men to write about their crimes, at least not for a while. But now I know, and this knowledge is the lens through which I see Eric. He is not merely an inmate interested in writing; he is a thrice-convicted drug dealer responsible for a woman's death. I see the weight of that—plus two decades of serious addiction—in his face. I read the regret, the despair of what he made of his life, of the lives he ruined. Is it enough, I wonder, to regret? To vow to do better? To serve your time? Suppose Mrs. Amerson had been my mother.

I can't think about that now with Eric standing in front of me, as I look at his quiet, troubled face and hear his desire to use writing as a way to keep himself accountable. He is here. I have to focus only on that. Eric helps me arrange metal folding chairs around the long, battered table that sits in the middle of the otherwise empty room. We're in one of the three rooms just down a short hall from the all-purpose room where I nervously delivered my come-to-the-writing-group speech a few months ago. Eric sits down just as Don, then Jimmie (a.k.a. Red), and finally Jann walk in. Mystery-man John is apparently going to continue to be a mystery.

I study Don (surreptitiously, I hope) as he sits with perfect posture, his face pleasant and composed. I am consumed with the wrong kind of curiosity—the slow-down-to-see-the-accident kind of curiosity—about what got him here. He looks like he could be a well-behaved white-collar criminal, maybe a forger or an embezzler (as if I know what they look like) and not someone who could commit an act of violence, not a murderer. Knowing about Eric, even though I did not pursue that knowledge, is making it harder for me to keep myself ignorant of other men's backstories. Especially Don's. Jimmie, with that tough-guy face, and Jann, with that swagger, fit some stereotyped, media-created picture I have of bad guys. Don does not.

I want to start the session with small talk to set a conversational mood. But the usual topics seem wildly inappropriate: the weather (to men who may not have had the opportunity to be outside all day, all week), the latest Facebook or Twitter silliness (to men who have no access to the internet, who were incarcerated before the internet existed), the latest movies (to men who have access only to what eventually shows up on nonpremium cable channels), vacations (of course not), family (too sensitive, too fraught). Food? Yes, that's a safe one. Tell me about prison food, I ask, and then I sit back and listen to a lively—and funny—fifteen-minute conversation liberally sprinkled with words like "greasy," "rubbery," and "tasteless." It sounds bad but possibly no worse than other institutional food. I think of the mushy, overcooked green beans, lumpy mashed potatoes, and gray meat I served to the old people in the care facility I worked at years ago. I think of the cardboard pizza served in my high school cafeteria. I join a conversation about how truly bad a truly bad cup of coffee can be. I am not looking to bond with these men, just create a somewhat relaxed atmosphere in the room. If I am going to ask them to share their lives with me, to write about their daily encounters, their fears and hopes, I need to find a tone for these meetings that is not pedagogical yet does include instruction, that is not therapeutic (I have no qualifications there) but posits writing as therapy, that invites openness but is not invasive. I need them to see me as both teacher and student. I do not want to be seen as an authority figure. They are surrounded by authority figures, by people who tell them what to do and when to do it. In fact, I want to get them to see the power *they* have when they write their own stories.

The teacher part of me launches into a little talk about how detail can make a moment come alive for a reader. I quote from the writing they've submitted to me during the past few months: how Jann doesn't just write that he drinks a cup of coffee in the morning but rather that he makes it with tap water from the small metal sink in his cell; how Jimmie doesn't just listen to music but scans the FM dial on his tinny radio for blues because he can't afford the $1.75 a song for the MP3 player; how Don doesn't just look out his small cell window but stares for hours at the traffic on Interstate 5, a mile distant. That's detail, I tell them. That's painting a picture with specifics. I talk about how detail depends on paying close attention, on taking the time to notice.

"I didn't really notice what I wasn't noticing until you had us do that 'week in the life' assignment," Don says.

"And there's more where that came from," I say, suggesting they write next about a friendship or significant relationship. I tell them it will be another two months until we can meet again, but that I continue to work on securing a regular once-a-month slot for us. I don't tell them that my efforts through existing contacts have stalled. "In the meantime," I say, looking at the four of them, "write."

—⁂—

In the meantime, I settle in for some serious reading on the history of prisons and the philosophy of incarceration. From the men, I hope to learn about the dailiness of prison life, but I also want to understand the how and the why of the world these men inhabit. How did prisons come to be, and why? What did—what do—we hope to accomplish by incarcerating people?

I'm surprised to learn that modern prisons (as opposed to castle dungeons) were actually a product of Enlightenment thinking, a humanitarian reaction to the cruel, painful, and degrading public humiliation of the punishments that then existed: whipping, branding, stoning, the pillory. Prison was, as Yale professor Caleb Smith has eloquently written, "the passage from spectacle of the scaffold to a secret discipline aimed at the soul." Punishment should not mark the body, thought the intellectuals and philosophers of the early nineteenth century; it should be etched into the psyche. For the wrongdoer, there needed to be ample time for regret, remorse, penitence, atonement—perhaps even redemption.

Thus in America was born a famous prison experiment, one that became, for a time, a model for others: the Eastern State Penitentiary in Philadelphia. In this product of Enlightenment thinking, each prisoner spent his entire sentence in solitary confinement, in virtually uninterrupted solitude and silence. There was no work, no communal dining or recreation, no activities of any kind. In the tiny, narrow stone cells that resembled the quarters of a medieval monastic order, the men were meant to examine their souls and come to a personal reckoning. Charles Dickens visited in 1842 and called the Pennsylvania facility a "living tomb." Although he thought the reformers meant well, he wrote, "I believe that few men are capable of estimating the immense amount of torture and agony which this dreadful punishment, prolonged for years, inflicts upon the sufferers."

Around the same time, in New York, an alternative system known as the Auburn model was evolving. In Auburn-style prisons, inmates did not spend twenty-four hours in their cells. They exited their cells every day to congregate in factory-like workshops where they created a variety of products, from barrels, boots, and harnesses to engines and boilers. The stated goal was to rehabilitate the men through hard work and industry. A result, intentional or not, was that the Auburn correctional facility became the first prison to profit from prisoner labor. While the prisoners worked, no interaction was permitted. The rule was not just absolute silence. Glances, hand signals, nods of the head—anything that could be construed as communication—were punishable by the whip. When they finished work, the Auburn prisoners returned to their solitary cells, locked down for the remaining hours. Dickens liked this "congregate system" better, writing that "[it] is, in its whole design and practice, excellent." Dickens might not have known that Elam Lynds, the legendary warden of Auburn who later oversaw the building of Sing Sing, called his inmates "coarse beings . . . who perceive with difficulty ideas and often even sensations."

I read about Zebulon Brockway, the "father of modern penology," who believed the mission of prisons was to promote compliant behavior among "inferior humans." I read about the criminologist Howard

Belding Gill, who in the 1920s took the opposite approach, developing a cooperatively governed "college-like community" at a Massachusetts state prison. I read Michel Foucault, who saw prisons as a mirror of modern "disciplinary society" built on power exercised through surveillance, obedience, and conformity. Then I turn to a big, thick "correctional policy and practices" textbook for the official version taught to those who want to become part of the system. What *is* the rationale behind incarceration? The textbook matter-of-factly lays out the purpose(s) of prison: incapacitation, deterrence, and retribution. But, I discover as I investigate further, incapacitation (preventing crime by removing and restricting the criminal) has its critics, who say that it works only as long as the person is in prison. The 70-percent-plus re-arrest rate of the previously incapacitated, reported by the Bureau of Justice Statistics, makes this point clearly.

About the positive effects of deterrence, there is, apparently, even less support. Prison sentences (particularly long sentences) are actually unlikely to deter future crime, according to research by Carnegie Mellon criminologist and statistician Daniel Nagin. Prisons, in fact, may have the opposite effect: Inmates learn more effective crime strategies from each other, and time spent in prison may desensitize many to the threat of future imprisonment. Time served is not as bad as they thought. It's hard to conceive of the prison experience as anything less than horrendous and unbearable, but the preincarceration lives of some of those who find themselves behind bars may have been almost equally as horrendous. For those of us (me, you) who don't live lives like that, it is beyond imagining that three hots and a cot (the food and shelter provided by a prison) might not be such a bad thing, that future imprisonment is less threatening than we imagine.

That leaves retribution, or, as the criminology text I'm reading so delicately puts it, "the exacting of a sacrifice on the part of the offender for the wrong done to victims and to society." It is the meaning of "exacting of sacrifice," the *operationalization* of "exacting sacrifice," that remains a subject of great debate. Except in the case of the death penalty, we no longer demand an eye for an eye, but we do demand a high price. Is that price the period of incarceration itself or the oftentimes physically, emotionally, and psychologically scarring life one lives while incarcerated?

Alexander Paterson, the British Commissioner of Prisons, is credited with saying, "Men are sent to prison *as* punishment, not *for* punishment." He and other reformers believed that it was the denial of freedom that was the punishment. The experience itself should not be torment.

Reformers believed in a fourth purpose for incarceration, a fourth mission: rehabilitation. "A man shall receive some definite training in habit and character," Paterson wrote in *The Prison Problem in America*. He proposed that men in prison should receive training and participate in games, that the goal of incarceration should be moral improvement, a long-lasting change in behavior and thought.

Rehabilitation did catch on. There were efforts to train prisoners for useful work that might translate into employment outside the walls. There were and are efforts, like those dating back to Howard Belding Gill's Massachusetts experiment, to bring educational opportunities— from GED classes to courses leading to bachelor's degrees—into prisons. Anger management classes, victim awareness seminars, twelve-step programs, and other self-help efforts became a part of some prisons. Therapists and counselors were hired by some institutions. But as early as the mid-1960s, efforts like these were already being politicized. Those who advocated for rehabilitation and the funds necessary to make it happen were being labeled as soft on crime. Arizona Republican Barry Goldwater, a powerful senator and presidential hopeful, used his political clout and national platform to toughen both the language and the policies surrounding incarceration. The rhetoric, as Caleb Smith writes in *The Prison and the American Imagination*, became "more openly vengeful and violent." Sentences were lengthened. Parole was less often granted. Funding for job training, education, and counseling was slashed. Tough-on-crime rhetoric and policies reached what many think of as a fever pitch with the passage of the Comprehensive Crime Control Act of 1984, a provision of which created a federal commission to establish mandatory minimum sentences for many crimes (thus erasing judicial discretion). In prisons, time off for good behavior became a thing of the past. Being tough on crime became synonymous with defunding rehabilitation efforts.

It is hard not to be deeply ambivalent about all this as I read. Of course bad guys need to be off the streets and out of my neighborhood. Crimes, most particularly violent crimes, crimes against people, need to be punished. But don't people, even people who do very bad things, deserve a chance to change? Why is it soft on crime to fund programs that can help them change?

"Prison," wrote Victor Hassine, "is a world more readily defined by what is missing than what is present." He meant the lack of freedom, privacy, personal agency, family, meaningful work. But he could also have been referring to the lack of rehabilitation efforts. Hassine, an accomplished author, a law school graduate, and a convicted murderer, committed suicide in prison shortly after being denied a commutation of sentence hearing. He had served twenty-seven years.

—⚏—

That world "defined by what is missing" is, for the men in my writing group, a very particular, insular world, a place with its own history and culture, its own policies and practices. Oregon State Penitentiary is one of more than seventeen hundred state prisons. State prisons are where upward of 80 percent of all those serving sentences are incarcerated. OSP is not the biggest prison in the country—that distinction goes to Angola (a.k.a. Louisiana State Penitentiary), with more than six thousand inmates—but with a population that hovers around twenty-two hundred, it is more populous than almost two-thirds of the towns in the state of Oregon. I will learn about life at OSP from those who have lived it for decades. But I can learn about its unique history myself.

The first and perhaps most disturbing thing I learn about OSP is about the so-called Oregon Boot, a shackle system developed and patented by the warden of the penitentiary back in the days just after the Civil War. At the time, the prison had a significant escape problem. Apparently the then-fourteen-foot-high wall was not enough of a deterrent. (Now the twenty-five-foot-high razor-wired concrete wall that surrounds the place extends down fifteen feet into the ground, making both over-the-wall and tunnel escape out of the question.) The solution to the escape problem in 1866 was a shackle consisting of a heavy iron band that locked around one ankle and was supported by another iron ring and braces that attached to the heel of a boot. The boot was placed on one leg only, keeping the inmate off balance and, after a while, in considerable pain. These shackles, manufactured by the prisoners themselves, weighed between five and twenty-eight pounds, and for a time, every prisoner was outfitted with one. If such a thing can be considered a claim to fame, OSP has at least one more: for three separate periods during the 1960s and 1970s, this place was home to Gary Gilmore, who, courtesy of Norman Mailer's tour de force nonfiction novel *The Executioner's Song* and the 1982 movie made from the book (Tommy Lee Jones played Gilmore), became the most cinematically famous prisoner since Bob Stroud, the Birdman of Alcatraz.

Another historical footnote uncovered: During World War I, the prison instituted an innovative daytime parole/honor system that released prisoners to work in outside jobs. Although the experiment was halted when almost half the work-released inmates failed to return, it led to the development of thriving in-prison industries, including what became, just a few years later, the largest flax-processing mill in the world.

The history of OSP, like the histories of most if not all prisons, is liberally sprinkled with escapes, thwarted escapes, riots, hunger strikes, protests, and other expressions of inmate anger, frustration, and dissatisfaction. The narrative may be commonplace, but it is still deeply disturbing. Nine prisoners were shot during a 1926 riot that began in the prison cafeteria. Seven hundred were involved in a 1936 riot—one died, two were wounded—in response to a court ruling that made it more difficult for prisoners to be released after serving their minimum sentence. In December 1951, inmates attempted a mass escape after receiving weapons from a sympathetic guard. The plan was foiled by an informant (who was quickly transferred to Folsom Prison for his own protection). Unrest continued through 1952 when more than thirteen hundred prisoners staged an eight-day hunger strike to protest the alleged brutality of a guard. Two months later, an escape attempt was suppressed with gunfire. The next summer a major insurrection erupted when more than a thousand prisoners, striking for better food and medical care, stopped working and barricaded themselves in the cafeteria. Ultimately the inmates gained control of most of the prison and started fires in the flax plant, laundry room, tailor room, and machine shop. Guards armed with tear gas, shotguns, and rifles finally subdued them, corralling eleven hundred prisoners outside in the baseball diamond without food or water for two days and a night.

Throughout the 1960s, prisoners continued to protest poor medical and dental care and limited visitation rights. Unrest culminated in
March 1968 in an uprising that began with the takeover of the prison's
control floor, that very same center space I walk through to get to the
activities floor. Some seven hundred prisoners took control of the prison,
started a fire in the flour shop, and held forty guards and prison employees hostage. Two inmates were stabbed during the riot. In November of
the same year, a work stoppage by eighty-one inmate laundry workers
was controlled by guards with clubs. And on it goes.

One OSP historical fact that stands far outside the riot-strike-escape
narrative is the story of Gene/Jean, a thirty-something prisoner who had
served three years on a morals violation and may very well have been
the first prisoner to undergo gender reassignment surgery behind bars.
The story of Jean's hormone treatments and two surgeries, published in the
Oregonian newspaper and picked up by the wire services, noted that
"a number of experts" believed that gender reassignment would aid in
Jean's rehabilitation. She was released soon after the surgeries. The year
was 1965.

Four

I'VE BEEN RUNNING THIS STILL-TO-BE-OFFICIALLY-sanctioned writing group under the radar for months now, our infrequent sessions unobtrusively piggybacked on other Lifers' Club events. In between times, I see their work when it manages to get to me. But now there's a new staffer on the activities floor, a man who is taking an interest in the writers' group. I am told that this guy is too new to trust, that he doesn't know the ropes, that I could endanger the future of the group by linking up with him, by going public. Best to stay in the shadows. The prison environment breeds paranoia, and not just among the inmates. The insulated hierarchy above, the turf-protecting minions below—these are institutional traits I know well from my time at universities. But I also know when to trust my gut, and my gut says this guy, Steven Finster, is the real deal.

We get acquainted first via email and then in an impromptu conversation while I'm waiting in the hallway before the next meeting of the writers' group. "Impromptu conversation" may not be the right way of putting this. Clearly we are sizing each other up. I am interviewing him without trying to make it seem as if I'm interviewing him. I've read the exposés of abusive, sadistic prison guards and uncaring prison bureaucrats. I've seen those movies. Steven is new to the activities job, but he's worked in the prison for years as a guard. I've read that some of the fiercest pushback to mounting enrichment and educational programs inside comes from guards and prison workers who see offerings like the writing group as unearned—and undeserved—special opportunities for the "bad guys." If Steven thinks like this, I want to keep my distance.

Meanwhile, standing in the hallway between the activities office and the room I use for the group meetings, he is interviewing me without seeming to as he tries to figure out if I am one of those starry-eyed, here-today-gone-tomorrow do-gooders—or worse, one of those women who get off on being around dangerous men. Maybe it's how direct he is, how he looks like a cross between an aging Hells Angel and Santa Claus, how easily he laughs, but I like him immediately.

It turns out that the end of the writers' group meeting coincides with the end of Steven's shift. We agree to go for coffee at a little café a few miles outside the walls. At first we talk a bit tentatively about books we're reading—a subject both safe and potentially revealing. He is a big fan of Ted Conover's prison book, *Newjack*, as am I. That's a good start. He tells me he is both a reader and a writer of poetry. "Honorable mention poetry," he says, laughing. "Nothing publishable." I tell him a little bit about my work. It seems we share not just a love of story but a belief in the power of story, its *curative* power.

"Stories, duct tape, and WD-40," I say, "that'll fix most anything." I say this to curry favor—he is clearly a duct tape and WD-40 kind of guy—but I also truly believe it. He nods his head and laughs, and the conversation becomes warmer, friendlier, and more animated. Steven refers to himself as a "rural Oregon redneck," who, true to type, dropped out of high school, married at seventeen, and then served in the navy for more than twenty years. But he is a study in paradox: He rides a motor-cycle and identifies with the Tea Party, but he is also a licensed practical nurse who once worked on a dementia ward. A high school dropout, he now holds two master's degrees, one in theology, the other in criminal justice. He is a seasoned prison officer who spends most of his time with convicted felons, but he believes in second chances. He believes in foster-ing opportunities for growth and change.

"I'm what they call a 'hug-a-thug,'" he tells me, laughing. He hap-pily embraces this meant-as-an-insult moniker. More important to me, he embraces and supports the writing group. He wants to help. At last I have an ally—a startlingly good-natured and relentlessly optimis-tic ally, two qualities not normally associated with people who work in prisons. As we leave the coffeehouse, talking about aging behind bars and the health issues the men face, he tells me that he's recently been diagnosed with MS. But he is "thrilled," he says, that he has the less debilitating relapsing-remitting variety of the disease. Now that is some serious silver-lining attitude. This man is a fifty-nine-year-old fireball.

When Steven comes into work the next day, he initiates the paperwork that begins an arduous four-step process to anoint me an official volunteer with my own ID badge. This will mean a streamlined procedure to get inside the prison. It will mean I won't need Steven, or some other officer, to leave his or her post to accompany me from the waiting room to the activities floor. This is a big deal. The fewer resources I use, the happier everyone is. Taking up an employee's time, even five minutes, counts against you (and your program), I've been told. Also I can bring in books and papers and take out the writers' work with me. No more back channels. No more depending on others. Even more important, it will provide legitimacy to the lifers' writing group because the meetings will be run by an *official volunteer*. The process, I discover, includes a multimodule online class, two half-day in-person trainings (each involving 120-mile trips for me), criminal checks, fingerprinting, and forms on top of forms. This is not going to happen quickly. But it is a huge step forward. Meanwhile, Steven says we can look at the activities calendar and start scheduling in regular *monthly* meetings for the group.

—◊◊◊—

At home I begin to study a copy of the OSP inmate handbook Steven gave me. It's the thirty-seven-page booklet distributed to all new inmates on arrival. These are the rules and regulations that govern their daily lives: where they live, how they dress, when they shower, when they eat, where they work, what property they can own. There are rules about how many books they can sign out from the prison library, how many religious services they can miss before their names are removed from that program, how many minutes they have to eat breakfast, what items can be on the floor of their cell, when they are allowed not to wear socks. Many actions require the submission of a "kite" (an internal inmate communication) or a form (or several) and a wait time (from a day to several months). This includes such things as ordering items from the canteen, requesting a book from the library, establishing a list of visitors, applying for "indigent envelopes" for those who can't afford the fifty-eight cents per envelope at the commissary.

Reading the handbook, page by page, rule by rule, I am struck by the meticulous management of the minutia of prison life. The handbook sets out an almost minute-by-minute daily schedule that begins with the 5:15 a.m. wake-up bell and is punctuated by bells and buzzers and head counts and lineups. It also seems to regulate all aspects of human behavior, regardless of how trivial, from how many pairs of socks you can own to how many pieces of fruit you can eat to how long you can talk on the phone. Little (if anything) is left to the individual to decide or act on. When you are trying to control the behavior of more than two thousand men who earned their place in prison by doing bad things and who really, really don't want to be there, this approach makes sense.

Yet I can't help but think that if you wanted to instill positive attitudes and the ability to make good choices, if you wanted to encourage what criminologists call "prosocial behavior" among two thousand men who will need to exhibit such traits to succeed outside of prison, then this militaristic micromanagement might not be the way to do it. All the prescriptions and proscriptions, the admonitions, the lengthy list of potential misconduct violations, the expectation of evildoing may be a path to what the psychologist Martin Seligman has called "learned helplessness." That's when a person (or an animal—Seligman's first experiments were on dogs) experiences and reexperiences a situation over which he has no control. There is no way to alter or have any impact on the situation. There is no action that can be taken to change the situation. This experience, repeated, teaches and then reinforces helplessness. It teaches that initiative and self-determination don't work. Not only that, but Seligman found that the person (or the dog) gives up trying, *even after* (as in the laboratory experiments) *the ability to take control is returned.*

Of particular interest to me as I read and reread the handbook is what is called the "Non-Cash Incentive Level Matrix," which is a three-tiered structure of privileges and opportunities for inmates based on their behavior. Essentially, the matrix incentivizes good behavior.

Privileges involve how much money they can spend in the canteen, which weight pile they can use to work out, how many hours a month they can see visitors, whether they can participate in various clubs, activities, or educational programs. There are three levels in the matrix. Level 3 is the top of the heap. Level 3 inmates can apply to live in A-block, the honor block. The cells are the same as in the other blocks, but Alpha block, as the men call it, has two tiers rather than five, making it quieter. Also, as it congregates the best-behaved convicts in one place, it is safer. That's what the A-block men in the writers' group tell me. There is less drama in A-block, they say. Because there are fewer incidents, they believe there is also less intense scrutiny by the guards, a small but palpable relaxation in the atmosphere, an ever-so-slight softening of inmate-officer interactions.

The men of level 3 don't usually break the rules. They have too much to lose: the opportunity to live in A-block (there is waiting list), the chance to participate in hobby shop (a popular perk for which there is a five-year wait), more time outside, access to educational opportunities, the ability to apply for leadership positions in clubs or special-interest groups. Membership in my writing group is another of these privileges. The men in the group, like all of the level 3 inmates, are invested in maintaining what the prison calls "clear conduct," which means not violating any of the ninety-one stated rules of misconduct. Most are what you would expect: injunctions against arson, assault, extortion, drugs, forgery, gambling, and anything and everything having to do with sex (including the possession of "unauthorized sexually explicit material," which leaves me wondering what the criteria would be for *authorized* sexually explicit material). No disrespecting guards. No contraband (including such diverse items as drug paraphernalia, pencil sharpeners, and uncanceled stamps). Section 2.06.01 is an injunction against "causing bodily fluids (human or animal) to come into contact with another inmate." Or, presumably, a guard. Later I learn from men in the group who have spent time in the hole (solitary confinement) that inmates sometimes fling their feces at guards.

I drive to the university to pick up another batch of papers from the group, hoping that with Steven's help, today might be the last time for this time-consuming arrangement. The envelope is the thickest yet. I am anticipating responses to homework I gave the group during our last session. I asked them to write about a friendship or a relationship that is important to them. I want to learn what kinds of relationships survive in prison. And I think, for them, the opportunity to write about a human connection in this place of isolation could be uplifting. The first paper I see is from Eric, neatly handwritten on loose-leaf paper. Seeing handwritten work continues to startle me. It looks like the assignments I submitted in high school. It reminds me not just that most of the men don't have access to computers but also that some of them have never used a computer, that none of them have ever held a smartphone in their hands, that our wired world is unknown to them.

Eric writes about a woman named Tara whom he calls "my significant other, common law wife, fiancée, best friend and soul mate." What follows is a hard-bitten, low-rent tale of drugs and addiction, drinking and partying, multiple marriages gone bad, near-fatal car wrecks, jealous boyfriends, jail, divorce, meth manufacturing, rehab, more jail. There's almost too much plot for one relationship. There's certainly too much drama. It's hard to believe that a relationship could survive what this one has: Eric's decades-long stretches in prison, Tara's two arrests and two stints in prison, her four children from four different fathers (none of them Eric). I read and reread and struggle to understand. When she was in prison, Eric wrote to her every day. She vowed to change her life. They both found religion. When she got out, he sent her money from his prison job to help support her children. He imagines a future together.

I read the pages for the third time. I don't know how to respond to the work. I want to help the men tell their stories, teach them how to actually craft stories—and this one is decidedly uncrafted—but how can I comment about the quality of the writing? There is too much pain and anguish in the story to think about offering suggestions on sentence structure or vocabulary. This man I hardly know has told me the most intimate of stories, an escalating chronology of terrible choices and their terrible consequences. This is not about his ability as a writer. It is about him struggling to understand his life. What I sense, therapist-without-portfolio that I am, is that Eric needs to have someone to help, to rescue, and Tara qualifies. His drug addiction and related crimes ruined his marriage. He cannot save that. He cannot bring back the life he took when he crashed into the car driven by the grandma out to do Christmas shopping. But maybe he can help balance the universe, or his soul, or karma; maybe he can restore and replenish what is good and moral inside him by "saving" Tara. Of course, I don't write that. (And, of course, I may be wrong.) Instead I write, "I am in awe of what you and Tara have been able to build and maintain. I am saddened to read about the life Tara has chosen to lead and simultaneously impressed by your acceptance, your quiet lack of judgment, and the consistent emotional (and financial) support you have offered."

There's also a handwritten piece from a man named Michael, a big, bearish guy with a shaved head, who showed up for one session early on and then disappeared. I assumed I wouldn't hear from him again. But he didn't quit the group. It turns out he was in the prison infirmary recovering from hip replacement surgery. In a separate note, he describes lying on his back for months in a "dark, dingy, dank room." He likens his experience in the infirmary to Hemingway's depiction of World War I–era hospitals. His tone is both intensely critical (he calls the place a "shit hole") and triumphant: "I made it back! For a while I didn't know if I was going to or not."

As his reentry to the group, he has submitted a piece on friendship, which begins as a treatise on betrayal. He writes about a cousin, a man he considered a best friend, who took the stand against him in Michael's murder trial. "He had a chance to clear some things up for me that day," Michael writes. But the cousin didn't. Michael doesn't stop there, blaming his cousin for not standing up for him. He blames himself for putting the man in such a position. Now in prison for more than a quarter of a century, Michael explains that he has learned to have "very very few friends." As I read on, I realize that it's not just trust, or lack thereof, that short-circuits prison friendships. It's almost the opposite. You find someone, a true friend. You open yourself up; you bond. Years go by. And then he leaves, his sentence served or parole granted, and is never to be seen again. It is the pain of that loss that keeps Michael from seeking deep connections. I am thinking about friendship and loss and how sensitive this man, Michael, is beneath the bluntness of his writing. And then I come to the end of the seven pages he has written. He signs his name, his full name, followed by his inmate number, which I am betting is just force of habit.

But I have his full name now. I didn't want to know it. I didn't want to be able to do what I do, what I knew I would do if and when I was privy to this information: I look him up on Oregon Offender Search. I Google him. I find a court of appeals ruling from the 1990s that details the crime that landed him here. Now I know that Michael drove over to the trailer where his estranged wife and two little girls were staying and stabbed her. Eleven times. I don't know what to do with this information, how to feel. Horrified, of course, but also confused: Is this man who came to class, who I am now remembering made a little joke about himself ("Hello," he said, introducing himself, "I'm the big bald guy"), who wrote about the pain of losing friends, is this the same guy who murdered his wife? When I see Michael again in a few weeks—I'm assuming he'll now start showing up for our sessions—which Michael will I see? Will I be able to look him in the eye? Will I fear him? When Eric wrote about the woman he killed, he detailed an act of vehicular homicide. It is not that the death of that woman is any less of a tragedy than the death of Michael's wife. But I can wrap my head around Eric's crime. He was high, he was eluding the cops, and something terrible happened. How do I understand what Michael did?

I put down the envelope with the rest of the submissions and go for a run. It's cold and rainy, a miserable day for a run. A mile in, the tips of my fingers turn white. I stay out too long, hoping to clear my head. Sometimes running helps. This time it doesn't.

I spend most of the evening reading through the remaining submissions, including two pieces—a total of twelve handwritten pages—from Don. The first is about his friendship with his neighbor on the cell block and begins with a deeply observant description of the man, his hazel eyes with flecks of green and blue that change depending on light, temperature, or mood; his graceful physicality that reminds Don of the Olympic diver Greg Louganis. Don describes the neighbor as "charismatic" with a "celebrity It factor." Everyone, writes Don, jockeys for this man's attention. "When I'm orbiting [his] planet, I'm suddenly funnier, smarter, better. . . . There's no win-lose with [him]. It's always win-win."

Don's other submission, an unassigned piece of work, offers an insight into how he has carefully constructed his prison life, how he propels himself forward with goals and has managed to live with hope during the past thirty-plus years of incarceration. It's presented matter-of-factly, but it is anything but matter-of-fact. It is, really, a stunning declaration of self-motivation, an extraordinary tale of *un*learned helplessness. I read about his successive five-year plans, a structure he developed for himself when he realized, during his first few years in prison, that his life was "all these broken pieces." He writes that he could not imagine how to live the long, long stretch ahead of him, so he decided to break it up into five-year chunks. During the first five years, he focused on education, earning an associate of arts degree from the community college that has a contract with OSP. He found enough upper-division classes offered by another university to earn his bachelor's degree. The next five years, he writes, were spent focusing on his mental health, on taking advantage of what was offered in counseling and therapy, by joining groups, by reading. He writes about what a challenge this was, how uncomfortable it felt to "turn myself inside out." But he emerged, he thinks, with healthier behaviors. He no longer feels "stuck in a dysfunctional circle."

The third five-year chunk was devoted to gaining new work skills in the prison industries and in saving some money. It seems from several convoluted paragraphs that the next five years were also spent on a variety of legal challenges to his sentence and to appeals to the parole board. I say "convoluted" not because Don writes confusingly but rather because the twists and turns of the legal and criminal justice systems are difficult to follow. The last five-year block he writes about is focused on raising his credit rating, taking classes and workshops on personal finance, exploring programs for first-time homeowners. He offers the name, phone number, and email address of the branch manager of the credit union he's working with—"this man has changed my life"—should I require any financial services. He writes that he has just finished reading Sheryl Sandberg's *Lean In* and is inspired by her story. He too wants to lean in.

Don's optimism about the future, his discipline and focus, is startling given his situation. But I wonder if maybe there are just people who make plans and people who don't, people who live life—inside or outside the walls of a penitentiary—by simply putting one foot in front of another and people who make lists and have goals and propel themselves forward. People who lean in. Don writes that he sees this writers' group as part of his "future trajectory," although he's not quite sure what that will be. "I've always thought about being released or paroled," he writes. "But had I been released earlier, then I wouldn't be here writing these words. I wouldn't be part of this group." I know what you're thinking because I think the same thing when I read this: he's sucking up to me. But when I put my prison paranoia aside, I realize that he has nothing to gain, nothing at all. I hold no cards in this game. I am forced to believe in his sincerity.

The next submission in the packet, neatly typed, carefully para-graphed, with subheads in bold, is from a man named Wil. Who is Wil? No one named Wil has attended any of our meetings or submit-ted any work up to this point. I start reading his "Week in the Life" account (I assume he learned of this early assignment from one of the regulars) that begins with a few biographical details, including the fact that he is seventy-eight years old. Okay, now I know who this is. This is the fierce, intimidating, flinty-eyed man I met briefly at the very first educational advisory board meeting when I presented the writers' group idea. I remember mostly that he stared hard at me and made me uncomfortable. I remember that he asked, in a tone I con-sidered a little threatening, "What's the purpose of this group?" after I thought I'd carefully explained that. I answered again, but I took the question as an indication that this guy did not trust me. And now, many months later, unrecruited, he has submitted a piece of writing. And it's good. It is direct, no-nonsense prose that reveals a keen eye and, surprisingly, a wry sense of humor. He chooses to focus on a single day. This is how he begins: "Today was typically atypical, and challenging. I awoke at 0400, performed 1000 abdominal crunches, 36 Hatha Yoga postures, 50 lunges, 50 pushups, 40 minutes of medita-tion and recitation, and ten minutes of Chi Kung. After examining my mirror for signs of arrested aging, I ate breakfast with 400 men most of whom I don't want to eat breakfast with. Client calls begin at 0715."

After I recover from the notion of a seventy-eight-year-old man (or, for that matter, a forty-eight-year-old man) performing this arduous predawn workout, after I wrap my head around the juxtaposition of his boot camp training–Hatha yoga regimen, I take a moment to marvel at the masterful writing, the precision, the understatement, the self-deprecating twist, the punch at the end. I feel the force of this punch— "Client calls begin at 0715"—as I read on to discover about his work as a crisis companion employed by OSP's Behavioral Health Services. He is on call 24/7 to help calm fellow prisoners in the throes of crises, men who present threatening, violent, or psychotic behavior. Many, he writes, suffer from PTSD. Some are veterans; others have experienced extreme domestic trauma.

About that first 0715 call of the day, he dispassionately notes: "A client has just tried to hang himself." In the single day he chronicles, Wil is called to help with three men, the man who tried to commit suicide, whom Wil describes as a twenty-four-year-old with an IQ of seventy; a Gulf War vet who served two tours as a gunner; and a third client who, Wil believes, tells him lies. "Phonies irritate me," he writes. "My time is finite." He leaves to teach a yoga class (he's been an instructor for seven years), lift weights for an hour, run three miles, and then sleep for six hours punctuated by startle responses, sweats, and teeth grinding. He, like most of his clients, suffers from PTSD. I don't know what motivated Wil to contribute, and I don't know if he'll show up to the group sessions—and if he does, I don't know how I will handle his intimidating presence, especially after reading his harrowing single-day take on the "Week in the Life" assignment—but I hope he decides to join. His perspective on prison life would be invaluable. I have much to learn from him.

The last paper in the stack is a single page from Jimmie, written in his perfect cursive hand. He apologizes for "falling off the globe." (Jimmie has been AWOL for the last two sessions.) He says that he broke a rib and, while laid up for a few weeks "meditating on my own stupidity," he heard back from the parole board. Back when the group first began, Jimmie was agonizing about writing his letter to the board. He managed to finish it, went in for his scheduled hearing, and then waited. And waited. Then came the response: the board denied him. The decision "crushed" him, he writes. He is just pulling himself out of deep depression. "It has been a real challenge not to just . . ." The dot-dot-dot is ominous. It implies, *more* than implies, thoughts of suicide.

I know that writing can't cure everything. But I also know it is possible to tell a story about what is happening in your life as a way to examine, and then move forward, in your life. I know it is possible to write your way through a crisis. Maybe Jimmie can do this.

Five

JIMMIE NEVER THOUGHT HE HAD A CHANCE. HE HAD LIFE without parole. He'd die in prison. But years ago, a jailhouse lawyer buddy of his said there might be a way. There might be some legal argument that could be made to force the parole board to at least give him a hearing. That was back in 1999.

Jimmie didn't believe he was worthy of parole. He believed (as he wrote in a little essay I assigned entitled "What Do I Think People Would Be Surprised to Learn about Me?") in an eye for an eye, a tooth for a tooth. He had murdered someone. He wasn't going to die for that crime, but he would spend the rest of his life behind bars atoning for it. And he figured that's what he deserved. As his father told him growing up—his alcoholic, physically abusive father—"Boy, if you step in shit, you're gonna get it between your toes."

Jimmie had been stepping in shit for most of his life. He was the sixth of nine children born to parents who would have had their kids removed if Child Protective Services had known what went on in that house. His parents screamed and fought with each other, not just with words but fists. The kids screamed and fought with each other. That was family life. Jimmie was born with what he calls a lazy eye, and from age five he wore Coke-bottle-thick glasses. For years he had to wear a patch over one eye. He was teased and bullied not just by his classmates but also (with the exception of one sister) by his own family. He grew up believing he was damaged goods. In writing about his childhood, he circles back to his lazy eye many times, tells stories about his lazy eye. Only once does he mention that age at six, his mother molested him.

He started cutting school in the first grade, hiding in the garage to avoid being picked on in class. At twelve he was riding his bike around town with three other boys, drinking beers stolen from their fathers ("I didn't like the taste," Jimmie writes, "but it gave me the courage to be myself"), smoking marijuana, breaking into abandoned buildings, and, in his words, "generally causing mayhem." By age fourteen he'd graduated to hard liquor, speed, pills, and sniffing glue. He'd distanced himself from the other boys in his childhood bicycle "gang" when they started dating and going to parties. Jimmie spent his time alone getting high. He remembers getting into some kind of trouble—he doesn't remember what kind (getting into trouble was what he did every day)—and his mother threatening to tell his father when he got home from his graveyard shift. Jimmie knew what that would mean. He remembers pleading with his mother not to "tell on me." He remembers lying in his bed, sleepless, until he heard the sound of crunching gravel as his father's car pulled into the driveway. He heard the house door open. He heard muffled conversation. Then he heard his father roar, "Jimmie, get in here." He wet the bed.

To pay for all the drugs he was consuming, he started committing petty crimes, break-ins, burglaries. Then crimes that were not so petty. At fifteen he was sent to "juvie," a juvenile justice facility. When he was released and back with his family, he dropped out of school, got into fights, and fashioned himself into a tough guy. For a couple of years, he writes, "I was the guy in the neighborhood everyone looked up to. My eye made no difference." Not long afterward, he was sentenced to a year in the county jail. After he was released, the trajectory of his criminal life continued, culminating in whatever landed him here, in a maximum-security prison, for the rest of his life. I don't know the specifics of those crimes. Jimmie told me when he first showed up to the writing group that if I knew what he did, I wouldn't let him in the group. "You probably couldn't even bear to look at me," he said.

Prison didn't change the life he was leading. He was tough, pugnacious, a fighter. It didn't stop his craving for drugs, his need to self-medicate his way out of the chaos of his life and the chaos that surrounded him. In fact, prison intensified those feelings. Now he knew, without a doubt, that he was, as he refers to himself back then, "a broken vessel" and "unfixable." He was twenty-one. He immediately began doing what convicts call "hard time," which means, as several of the men in the group have told me, "letting time do you rather than you do time." It means letting the circumstances of your incarcerated life dig a groove into your soul. "I baptized myself into the hustle of the convict life" is how Jimmie describes this time in his life, now more than thirty-five years ago. He immersed himself in drugs—"I stayed loaded at least fifty percent of the time"—smuggling, dealing, gambling, pumping iron, and "being aggressive toward my captors." He quickly became the trouble-making, trouble-seeking prison thug whom convicts call a yard dog. He racked up forty-eight major misconduct reports.

Once, during a disciplinary hearing, the adjudicator told him, "You have one of the most criminal minds I've ever met." Jimmie took this as a compliment. He went out of his way to taunt an officer assigned to the prison's drug task force who had Jimmie squarely in his sights. "I'm as high as a kite," he told the guy, making a show of his bloodshot eyes.

During those first few years behind bars, Jimmie spent half his time in solitary confinement, the hole. "The bucket" is what he calls it. When he wasn't in solitary, he was often on what is called "restrictions," which meant he was forbidden from going to the yard or having a job, activities the authorities (rightly) considered opportunities for Jimmie to make drug connections. He remembers one day, during one of his many confinements in solitary, a captain approaching his cell and looking hard at him through the bars. "You've turned into a fucking animal," the captain said. And Jimmie writes that he heard the truth of that, and for the first time in years, that night in his cell, he cried. Sitting in solitary confinement for so long with nothing to do but think, read, and write letters, he says he was forced to contemplate the path his life had taken. The path he had chosen. I hesitate to write anything good about solitary confinement. There is so much evidence, so much damning research concerning the psychological and emotional consequences of caging a human being in a stripped-down cell for twenty-three hours a day with no human contact. But Jimmie says solitary, because it offered no escape from the darkness of his life, was the beginning of his road back.

It would be nice now to chronicle a tough but ever-upward narrative of redemption. But sometimes insight does not immediately translate into action. Sometimes it takes years. And slaps upside the head. And punches to the gut. And multiple aha moments. After that night in solitary, Jimmie kept using drugs even as he participated in twelve-step programs. He kept using drugs even after one of the men with whom he shared needles told him he had AIDS. Jimmie got tested, was miraculously negative, and kept using. Requesting the test meant he had to participate in drug treatment services, where he met a mental health counselor. She gained his trust, he writes. She gave him good advice, he writes. He told her he'd stop using needles. He didn't.

His activities, his anger, his hard-time approach to life in prison continued to land him in segregation. His older sister, the one sibling he was close to, the one who didn't tease him about his lazy eye, traveled a long distance to see him. While she was boarding the plane in California, he was being escorted, yet again, to the disciplinary unit for a dirty-urine analysis. They were able to visit, but only for thirty minutes and separated by a glass partition. She was angry and hurt. He told her, with the best of intentions, that he was done using drugs. Within hours, he was high again. During another visit while he was in the hole, his father brought in Jimmie's young daughter from a brief early marriage. When I read about this visit in one of Jimmie's essays, I was struck by the fact that, although chronicling his past in great detail, he had never mentioned the marriage or the daughter. But she appears in this scene. Separated by thick glass, speaking by telephone, they visit. At one point the little girl asked him, he remembers, "Daddy, am I ever going to be able to hug you again?" The words tore at his heart, he says. Of course they did. He promised her that she'd never have to visit him through a glass partition again, which meant he wouldn't be sanctioned, which meant his urine wouldn't test dirty, which meant he would stop using. Within days, he was high again. To someone who has never been an addict—me, perhaps you—this is almost incomprehensible. But every addict, and anyone who has studied addiction, understands the way it takes hold and won't let go. Jimmie had come to prison in 1980. He didn't stop using until 2003.

When the moment came, it came in a flash. He describes it that way. He was sitting at a table across from a buddy with whom he'd done multiple drug deals. The guy was wanting to arrange another deal, a smuggling operation. To tempt Jimmie, he slid over a fifty-dollar paper of heroin. Yes, this is happening in prison. In maximum-security prison. That's when Jimmie says he heard a voice, an internal voice that was so real and so convincing that he thought then, and still believes, that it was God talking. It's common—a cliché even—for a prisoner to say that he has "found God." The multitude of twelve-step programs in prisons all reference and are based on the notion of acknowledging and accepting a higher being. And if ever there was a time to believe in a higher being who watched over you, cared about you, and would forgive you for whatever you did, sitting in a prison cell facing a long life of sitting in a prison cell would be that time. It is also true that "I found God, and now I am a changed man" can be a contrived narrative, a crowd-pleaser. Jimmie never drank the twelve-step Kool-Aid, and he is unflinchingly, brutally, honest about his many faults, transgression, and offenses. So maybe it was God. I believe Jimmie believes it was. But whether it was divine intervention or his long-dormant conscience poked so often that it finally awakened, what he heard was, "Jimmie, it's time to stop." And he *heard* it, and he knew it was true, and he knew it was time. What he had resisted taking seriously in AA and NA, what he had ignored during his counseling sessions, the AIDS scare, the empty promises he made to his sister, his daughter—all of those voices he had been deaf to—he now heard. He was going to clean up his act. And he was going to stay clean.

Was it hard? Jimmie had been an addict since he was a kid. In prison, staying high was an escape from his surroundings and from himself, from his dark past, from the knowledge of what he had done. Weed and heroin and whatever else he could get his hands on dulled the pain. So of course it was hard. Jimmie comments only on the recurring waves of depression that threatened, still threaten, to drown him. But he pushed through. He sought out drug, self-help, anger management, and victims' awareness programs. His involvement started, he admits, as a means to fill the space in his head, to "crowd out thoughts of my wasted life." But he kept showing up, and he listened, and he learned. He learned about how family behaviors shaped his worldview, how anger is an emotion that can be controlled, what addiction does to the body and the mind. And he thought, for the first time, about doing something useful in prison. Life without parole did not have to mean life without purpose. He joined the prison's hospice program, where inmate volunteers sit with dying men in a section of the in-house infirmary. He worked for the mental health department, called in to sit on suicide watches. He stopped doing hard time.

And then he met Donna.

Donna had a son who had recently been sentenced and was serving time at OSP. She was scared for him. She asked someone she knew who inside the walls might look out for her son, who could be trusted, and Jimmie was the name she got. So she wrote him, and he agreed to watch out for the kid. They started corresponding, sporadically at first, centered on her son. But then the letters became longer—eight, ten, twelve pages—and more frequent. They became personal. Donna was in crisis. Her son was a criminal. What had she done wrong? "How does it feel to have raised a monster?" someone in her town asked her. She didn't know what to do with the pain or how to talk about it. She found a sympathetic ear in Jimmie, a person who could listen without judgment, a person on intimate terms with pain and shame. He found a connection, not a fellow con to whom he had to present a mask, not a family member bowed under the weight of all that family baggage, but someone new. Jimmie says they both needed someone in their lives whom they could trust with their respective pain. He says Donna became the "normalcy" he believed he had lost forever because of his sins, and he became the "energy" that pulled her out of her darkness.

For months, they wrote. Then they started speaking on the phone. Jimmie was scared, tongue-tied, but it got easier. She was easy to talk to. Soon they were discussing the idea of actually meeting face-to-face. But it wasn't going to be that easy. Donna was already on her son's visiting list, and the Department of Corrections has a policy stating that a person cannot be on two inmates' visiting lists unless the person is related to both inmates. I'm sure that's not an arbitrary rule. It is probably meant to prevent nefarious back-channel communication, gang-related activities, or some other threat. But it was a real problem for Donna and Jimmie. Donna could not visit both her son and Jimmie, and she would certainly not remove herself from her son's list to be on Jimmie's. They came up with a plan. They would arrange to be in the visiting room at the same time, she seeing her son, Jimmie visiting with his father. They preplanned to sit in the same area. The room itself is large with chairs, couches, and tables arranged for separate conversation. Cross talk was a violation of the rules, but if they were careful, they might get away with it.

Over the years Jimmie hadn't paid much attention to his appearance, but the day of the visit he shaved, got a haircut in the prison barber shop, and put on his "best" prison blues. When he writes about this first meeting, he sounds like a kid—although certainly not the felonious, streetwise kid he had been—and not a man in his midforties. She is sitting with her son catty-corner to where his father and stepmother are sitting. He thinks she is even more beautiful than the picture she sent. They have never met, but they are not strangers. What they have revealed to each other in six months of letters and phone calls is more than most couples reveal in years, or ever. He can barely pay attention to his own visitors. The two of them flirt with their eyes. Then, like a kid, he writes her a little note and has his stepmother pass it over surreptitiously. The note passing is pure grade school, but the message inside is bold: "Do you love me check yes or no." He has drawn two little boxes. The note comes back via stepmother. When he opens it anxiously, he sees that she has drawn a third box, "maybe," and checked that one.

They write and talk on the phone, still trying to figure out a way they can have regular visits. If he puts in for a transfer to another prison, she could be on his visitor's list there, but this would mean a much longer drive for his ailing father. So they scotch that idea. Jimmie has another idea, grand, almost preposterous: They could get married. Then Donna could visit both her son and her husband. She says yes.

When Jimmie mentioned in passing that he had a wife—he referred to her in that very first writers' group meeting—I thought, Who would stay married to a man serving a life without parole sentence? I assumed they had been married before he came to prison and that she must be the most loyal, saintliest, and most steadfast wife ever. But Jimmie told me they didn't know each other on the outside, that they had gotten married in prison, in the visiting room. And so I thought, before I knew anything more about the relationship, What kind of a woman would choose to marry a convicted murderer with whom she will never have a shared life?

I couldn't get the answer by meeting Donna, even if she agreed and Jimmie gave his blessing. If it became known that I had contact with the families or friends of the men in the writing group, I could lose the privilege of coming into the prison. Instead I looked for the answer, or at least a hint of an answer, elsewhere. I found it in Megan Comfort's sensitive and thought-provoking study of women who love men who are in prison, *Doing Time Together*. The book is an analysis of her observations and in-depth interviews with fifty women whose male partners were serving time in San Quentin. Her findings at first took me by complete surprise. But then as I thought about them, they made so much sense that I was surprised at my own surprise. Here she is, writing like the PhD sociologist she is: "Wives . . . adapt their romantic expectations to carceral realities and recast their relationships as benefitting precisely from the strictures that contain and control their mates."

What that means is that wives appreciate the authoritarian prison regime that shapes their husbands' behavior, that suppresses angry responses, confrontation, violence, and for many, their drug use. Simply put, their husbands behave better inside than out, and the wives like that. They are attracted to that. The wives Megan Comfort interviews praise their partners for, as she writes, "a range of stereotypically feminine qualities—intensive communication, attentiveness to the relationship, expression of emotion." Later, she writes, as if she had been a fly on the wall observing Donna and Jimmie's courtship by correspondence, that men in prison become "highly communicative and expressive in their confinement" and that women "take pleasure" in this. So it is not pity or desperation or a fascination with "bad boys" that brings women, or at least some women, into the lives of incarcerated men. It is just the opposite. It is that in prison, a woman can find an introspective, communicative, well-behaved man who values and nurtures an emotionally intimate relationship, perhaps in part because physical intimacy is not possible. And she always knows where he is. And it's not her responsibility if he derails.

Donna and Jimmie decide to marry. And, of course, it is not easy. Nothing in prison is easy.

—⚮—

For Donna and Jimmie to get married, DOC rules stated that Jimmie would have to be on his future wife's guest list first—which makes sense—but which meant, as the rules stated, she would have to be removed from her son's list. Once removed from her son's, it would take a month for her to get approved for Jimmie's list, and then another month before they could get married. The problem was that Donna was not just visiting her son, she was also bringing her son's children in to see him. To give up both her own visitation and her commitment to preserving the relationship between her son and his young children was too much to sacrifice. Again Jimmie contemplated putting in for a transfer to another prison. But suppose he and Donna didn't work out? Then he'd be stuck at the other prison, hundreds of miles away from his family, until he could once again put in for a transfer—which might or might not come through.

As a last-ditch attempt before applying for the transfer, he requested a meeting with one of the prison's assistant superintendents. It's hard to overemphasize what a Hail Mary move this was. DOC rules, policies, and procedures are, if not etched in stone, written in almost indelible ink. At the bottom of the prison hierarchy sits the virtually powerless prisoner; at the top, the virtually untouchable administrators. Jimmie considered it a certifiable miracle that he was granted a meeting. The administrator, Amy Pinkley-Wernz, listened patiently, and she cared. She agreed to bend the rules and allow Donna to be on both visiting lists for a month before the wedding. Jimmie was astonished, but he recovered sufficiently to ask for something more: "How about two months?"

"Why do you need the extra time?" she asked.

Jimmie slid his chair a little closer to her desk and leaned in. "For romance, Ms. Wernz," he said. She smiled and granted the request.

A wedding in prison is not remotely akin to a wedding in what incarcerated men always refer to as "the free world." For starters, you can't choose your own date: weddings take place only two days a year, once in April, once in October. And, of course, you can't choose the venue: weddings take place in the OSP visitors' room. It might be that you can choose your own officiant, but the institution recommended a certain man, Reverend Cooper, who apparently conducted virtually all of the ceremonies. He charged twenty dollars a pop. The couple could not write their own vows. Guests? From the groom's side, only ten were allowed, and they had to be on Jimmie's approved visiting list. No food.

No flowers. The groom would be dressed in prison blues. And, needless to say: no honeymoon.

Still, it would be an occasion with a capital O. They requested to be the first of the three scheduled weddings that day. Eight in the morning is not prime wedding time, but a buddy had told Jimmie that if you were married first, you got to stay around in the visitors' room until the other two couples went through their ceremonies. Those forty extra minutes would be the closest to a honeymoon they'd get.

Donna entered wearing a long blue dress and white high heels. The groom, in OSP-stamped denim, noted that he suffered heart palpitations and a dry mouth. The bride was given away by her son, the one to whom they owed their relationship. None of her other family members attended. They were, as Jimmie understated, "not too keen" on the idea of the marriage. Jimmie had his father, stepmother, his daughter from that early first marriage (now grown), and her husband. When I read that Jimmie invited his father—the man who beat him as a child, the man he so feared that fourteen-year-old Jimmie wet his pants in anticipation of an encounter—I could barely believe it. I had been equally stunned that the father visited semiregularly. Had they forgotten their past? Had they forgiven each other? The wedding party, five plus the couple, assembled at 8:15 a.m. on October 26, 2004. The couple stood under what Jimmie described as "a plain white plastic arch with no flowers." Reverend Cooper was, as Jimmie writes, "on the clock," and the ceremony was quick and by the book. But the reverend was not immune to the underlying joy of the moment. Jimmie remembers his wit and humor. But mostly he remembers the kiss. He remembers the pure elation, not merely of the physical contact but of the knowledge that, although he had long ago given up any thought of having someone love him, this woman loved him.

Not too long after the marriage, they were talking on the phone. Jimmie was unusually quiet and withdrawn. When Donna asked why, he explained to her that there was this legal brief a prison buddy had worked on several years back; the guy was now transferred, and Jimmie didn't know what to do. The brief the guy was putting together, as Jimmie understood it, rested on what might be a very thin legal distinction. The court had actually sentenced him to life, not life without parole. It was the parole board that had used one of its rules to deny him the possibility of parole. Could the parole board be compelled to grant him a hearing?

"I thought you didn't have a chance to get out," Donna said.

Jimmie had told her just that when they first started corresponding and had never mentioned this idea his buddy was working on. He didn't want her to be under "any delusion," as he put it, that they could have a real life together. And this chance was so remote, Jimmie thought, that he didn't want to raise any hopes. Now, however, there was a future worth imagining and fighting for, a future with Donna. And so for the next several years, Donna spent thousands of dollars in attorney's fees to see if it would be possible to get Jimmie a hearing. For the past several years, he had thrown himself into every alcohol and drug program, therapeutic workshop, educational opportunity, church seminar, and volunteer activity he could because, in his words, "I saw the monster I had become, and I knew I was responsible for my change . . . I had to make amends." Now his involvement continued, but his focus shifted. Now he was doing all those things to prove to someone *else* that he had changed. Now he was amassing evidence for the board.

Once, during this decade-long attempt, the attorney wrote Jimmie a letter saying that the board agreed to a hearing and that he would flag Jimmie's file and get back to him when the date was set. Jimmie says the euphoria "spread through my veins like good liquor." He called Donna. They cried. They celebrated.

When six months went by without a word, Jimmie put in a call to the attorney. A week later he got a letter from the attorney that stated in part: "I called the hearing scheduler, and I am grieved to tell you that the Board said they made a mistake and you don't have a hearing coming."

That's it, Jimmie thought. I cannot put myself or Donna through this anymore. I have caused my loved ones enough sorrow for a lifetime. I'm giving up this fight.

Donna urged him to do one more thing. She talked Jimmie into writing a personal letter to the board explaining the journey he had been on since incarceration and the changes he had made. Jimmie procrastinated for a full year. Finally, in the summer of 2011, he forced himself to write a nine-page letter and sent it off, even though he figured there was "not even a sliver of hope" that anything would come of it.

But something came of it. In May 2013 Jimmie heard that he had been granted a hearing for October of that year. In his cell were stacks of material, boxes with reams of paper, proof of his activities, proof that he had done everything he could to rehabilitate himself, to redeem himself, to change himself from murderer to a man worthy of a life outside of prison. He was fifty-four. He had been in prison since he was twenty-one.

The board did not grant him parole that fall. But neither did it close the door. In fact, board members praised Jimmie for all he had accomplished. They encouraged him to seek further counseling, continue with the programs in which he was already enrolled, and come back for another hearing in two years. This, in prison slang, is being "flopped." It wasn't a flat denial. It might even be considered good news. The next time, in two short years, he had a real chance of being paroled. That's what he and Donna thought.

—⁓—

The second hearing was scheduled for the end of 2015. This was a few months after I started the writers' group. I was just getting to know Jimmie. He had shown up for a few meetings, submitted some work, then disappeared. Later I would learn that he'd had his second hearing, that the board had told him he didn't have the right to a hearing, that there would be no more hearings, that there would be no parole. Ever.

That's when Jimmie says that he went back to doing hard time.

He tried, he writes, to go back to being the tough guy he used to be, the yard dog who knew how to survive. He got in several fights and was laid up in bed for a few weeks with a cut jaw and what he thought were broken ribs. He couldn't go to the infirmary. There'd be questions to answer. So he laid on his bunk in his cell and thought about the years ahead of him. When he was mobile again, he started asking around about scoring heroin. But he was out of the mix for so long—he had been clean for a dozen years—that he no longer had connections. He ended up asking a guy who knew Donna's son, and Donna's son told his mother. Donna never told Jimmie that she knew he'd been asking around for heroin. She just told him she believed in him.

Back in his cell, he grappled with the depression he had fought most of his life. He felt claustrophobic, but when he thought about going out onto the tier, he was overcome by anxiety, afraid he couldn't control the tears, afraid to show weakness. A week later he was still spending hours sitting on a tote box in front of his bunk reeling from the board's decision. He looked at the row of books and pamphlets on his shelf, the self-help manuals, the journals, the cognitive-behavioral guides that filled a plastic box under his bed. This was the paper trail that marked his journey, the evidence that he had made that journey.

He took down the books and manuals and pamphlets. He opened the box filled with stacks and stacks of handwritten papers, and one by one, page by page, he tore each into little pieces. He tore up everything and piled it high on his cot. The trash—he thought of it as trash—represented years of working on his rehabilitation. At first the work was entirely self-motivated, but he knew, after he caught the whiff of freedom, after the possibility of a parole hearing emerged, that his motivation had changed. His focus became external. He was jumping through hoops, that's how he put it, for the parole board. And he was finished doing that. He understood (and it is clear in his writing about this that he reveled in) the irony: It was the board slamming the door on the possibility of freedom that freed him. He would start living for himself again, reading what he wanted to read, doing what he wanted to do, making his own choices. He stopped going to all the groups he had joined, stopped going to all the meetings.

I didn't know any of this at the time. All I knew is that Jimmie had disappeared from the writers' group, and I didn't know if I'd ever see him again.

Six

MY NEW OSP ALLY, STEVEN, IS WORKING TO FIND MONTHLY slots in the calendar to slip in the writers' group, but what we both want is for the group to have its own identity, to be officially sanctioned. That means a formal proposal to Steven's boss, the administrator in charge of correctional rehabilitation, which includes all of the prison's programs, activities, clubs, and education. This is Ms. Pinkley-Wernz, the same Ms. Pinkley-Wernz (as if there could be two) who smoothed the way for Jimmie and Donna to get married. This gives me hope. Also Steven thinks highly of her.

I spend hours crafting and polishing the proposal. I want it to be short and powerful, to show specific benefits, to use some of the language of corrections and incarceration so as not to challenge too much. Clarifying and articulating those objectives, putting them down on paper, turns out to be more challenging than I imagined, considering that I presented a version of these very ideas to the prison education group many months ago, that I spoke to the Lifers' Club promoting the group and its objectives many months ago, and that I have been leading the group for months based on these objectives. But this proposal is for a very different, much tougher audience. When I come in for the next shoe-horned-into-the-calendar meeting, Steven tells me he has forwarded the proposal to his boss and that last week he introduced it at a staff meeting.

"I told them, 'Hey, you have a writer here, a real writer, and she's coming in, volunteering, and the guys are really getting something from it. How can you say no?'"

We look at each other and burst out laughing in unison. *How can they say no?* Well, no is the default answer. We both know that. But we're moving forward anyway. More than the strength of the proposal itself, more than the track record the group is just beginning to establish, a yes to the proposal may depend on Steven's assertion that the group will be, in the vernacular, resource neutral. At the staff meeting, and in his own addendum to my proposal, he made clear that there would be no extra work for anyone, a major sticking point for any new activity. The group would be scheduled for when Steven was already on duty. And, Steven told them, I was starting the process to get my own ID badge, which would mean I would need no special handling or attention when I came into the prison.

—⁂—

And so I start down the long road—an even longer road than I expected—to become an official OSP education volunteer. The first step is easy, if a bit unsettling: filling out a ten-page application. The first few pages ask for basic information (name, address, DOB, driver's license number) that will make it easy to run me through the criminal database system. But from page 4 on? That's where the unsettling stuff starts. I have to sign a waiver of my right to sue should any accident or injury happen while I am volunteering. (Not to worry though; the DOC has "limited Accidental Death and Dismemberment" coverage for me should I become accidentally dead or limbless.) I have to sign another waiver about the extent of my civil liability. I don't know what that means, but I sign it. I have to sign a professional ethics statement, which states I must "value and maintain the highest ideals." I am delighted there is such a statement. I am not quite as delighted to read this sentence: "To the best of my ability I will remain calm in the face of danger and maintain self-restraint in the face of scorn or ridicule." I sign that page before I can think too much about "danger," "scorn," and "ridicule." There's a page and an addendum devoted to PREA—this place is all about acronyms—the Prison Rape Elimination Act, about which, it turns out, I will hear much, much more in my three-part training. Right now the descriptive title is both sufficient and ominous. I have to initial and sign in two places. I attach a four-page resume to accompany the application.

And then I wait. And wait. For me to begin the first part of my train-ing, a five-part online learning module, the DOC's volunteer coordina-tor has to read through my application, approve it, send me a link to the training site, and set up a temporary password. She is on vacation. Then she is back from vacation and slammed with work. Then my application mysteriously disappears. I find this out after a month goes by without hearing anything. I call her. She is friendly and apologetic. Apparently there are twenty-six hundred active volunteers in the DOC system, and she tracks all of them in one way or another. I resend all the material. She processes it. Finally, close to two months after sending in the application, I can begin the training by logging in to a special website. But to navigate my way through the site, I must first read the accompanying fifteen-page guide. Should a site be so complicated that it requires a fifteen-page guide? This is a rhetorical question.

Each learning module requires me to read screens and screens of DOC documents, policies, rules, and regulations and then answer a series of multichoice questions about what I've just read. If I answer (mostly) correctly, I can proceed to the next module. I know how to take tests. I ace all but one module. The evidence of my competence is electronically communicated to the coordinator, who then sends me an email invitation to the first of two in-person training sessions, which are generally held once a month but sometimes not. I have to wait two months for the next scheduled one.

—⁓—

The all-afternoon NSP (nonemployee service provider) training is held in a small conference room in an old State of Oregon building called the Dome (because it has one). A veteran DOC administrator named Nichole Brown is running the show. There's much confusion for the first twenty minutes as she struggles with tech incompatibility issues and encounters problems with the livestream from two distant prison locations where other NSPs will be participating remotely. In the confu-sion of getting the system to work, we all of a sudden see video from the Snake River Correctional Institution superintendent's office, where he is sitting at his desk, talking on the phone, and conducting daily busi-ness. He doesn't know we can see him, and for a moment that stretches into two or three, Ms. Brown can't figure out how to cut the feed. I hold my breath wondering if he's going to do what any normal person might do when he has no reason to believe others are looking: pick his nose, scratch some part of his body. He doesn't. I exchange glances with the other volunteer in training in the room, a man who runs a weekly AA meeting at a medium-security correctional facility in Salem. We want to laugh, but we don't.

It turns out that the training session is not really a *training* session but rather a PowerPoint journey through the organizational structure, goals, and management policies of the state's DOC. Simultaneously fascinating and soporific, the presentation is an insight into a big, lumbering bureaucracy made even more opaque than it probably is by the organization's insistence on acronyms for just about everything (CCM: Correctional Case Management; OAM: Oregon Accountability Model; STM: Security Threat Management; BHS: Behavioral Health Services . . . and so forth). Ms. Brown is reading from a script, with us following along from our own twenty-nine-page photocopied packet, which is, in fact, her script. An hour in, and I wonder if it's okay to interrupt with a question. Another two trainees have joined our small group, and no one but Ms. Brown has said anything. But the slides she's showing refer to prison inmates using yet another acronym, AICs—adults in custody—a phrase I've never heard before, and I'm curious. What happened to "inmates," "prisoners," "convicts"? AIC seems both clunky and oddly euphemistic. I ask. Ms. Brown appears happy to stop reading from the script for a moment. She explains that AIC is, indeed, the way the system now refers to inmates. The director of corrections decided to change the language to "humanize" the inmates. "We ask you to use this term as well," Ms. Brown says, making eye contact with each of us in turn. Also she says that prison guards are no longer referred to as guards. They are called corrections officers.

Ms. Brown has worked for the DOC for seventeen years and has given this training she doesn't know how many times. When she reads from the script, she is obviously on autopilot. But she interrupts her recitation at one point, and her demeanor changes. "I have to tell you," she says, leaning forward, her palms flat on the conference table we are all gathered around, "some people go through this training, but they get in trouble."

Getting in trouble is doing something against the rules. You lose your access if you do something against the rules. You lose your ID badge, the golden ticket. Or worse. In a stern voice very much unlike her script-reading voice, she lists the rules that, presumably, have tripped up others: "Anything you bring in with you has to be okayed by your supervisor. Anything you bring in has to come out. Ask permission; don't assume." She repeats this. "Don't provide services to those released from prison who you provided services for inside. And don't"—she hesitates—"get involved."

She tells us about a volunteer yoga instructor who fell in love with an adult in custody and had a relationship with him when he was released. Apparently it was then discovered that there had been "intimacy" prior to release. The yoga instructor is facing criminal charges.

This anecdote introduces what to me is the most disturbing part of the afternoon's training, the presentation focused on inmate manipulation. "That's right," says Ms. Brown, "I am now going to use the word 'inmate.'" She is using that word to show she is not giving respect to the manipulators. There are seven slides on inmate manipulation, each one more harrowing than the next. It's all about being suspicious of the inmates you work with. They may be grooming you. If they say you are great or the class is great, they may be setting you up to ask you for a little favor that becomes bigger and bigger until, this downward narrative goes, you are carrying in drugs for them. Or something like that. I immediately think of Don, who responded to my fill-in-the-blank prompt "The best part of my week was . . ." with "writing for Lauren." Is Don is grooming me? Should I be suspicious of every kindness? (Michael asks if I want a cup of coffee.)

One slide shows the multistep process of manipulation that proceeds this way: They observe you. Then single you out. Then they fish to see if you take the bait (do a small favor that seems innocuous). Then they up the ante, small favor by small favor. And then they've got you: You are compromised. They can hold the favor-granting over your head (you broke the rules, and they will rat you out) to extract even riskier favors.

The way you prevent this, according to what is undoubtedly hard-won DOC wisdom, is by never sharing any personal information with inmates because they can use that to get to you. I think about the fact that the guys are reading my book of essays on the art of writing. It is about the craft of nonfiction storytelling, which is why I brought it in for them to read, along with a few other writing books okayed by Steven. But many of the essays begin with a personal experience to illustrate the writing challenge. There's information about my family, the summer camp I went to, places I've lived.

"Any information can be helpful for a sting," Ms. Brown says. Inmates can get family or friends on the outside to find you on Facebook. (There is no internet connectivity with the outside world within the walls of OSP.) She tells us that she doesn't have a Facebook account nor any other social media presence. I sure do. It would be *very, very* easy to find out *lots and lots* about me. These past months I have been focused on getting the men in the group to trust me. Now all of a sudden I am thinking, Should I trust them?

I interrupt to ask a question. I have to ask about the Lifers' Club writers' group and how much of this "be suspicious of everything" advice I need to take to heart. She says that DOC "trains to the highest risk level," which is "probably not where these guys are." These guys—"They're level three, right?" she asks—they have too much to lose. "They model prosocial behavior," she says. "They know the ropes, and they don't want to get in trouble." Which I guess means that they don't want to get *me* in trouble either. I am comforted, but I remain queasy about all the personal information they can glean from my book of essays.

The next set of slides is about being taken hostage. I really, really do not want to think about this. It is not that it hasn't crossed my mind when I come into the prison. In fact, the officer who accompanies me and the other visitors without official IDs through screening and through two checkpoints and two locked gates has to deliver the this-is-a-dangerous-place-and-bad-things-could-happen-to-you disclaimer every time, like reading our Miranda rights. It never stops being disturbing to hear this, but I tell myself that the men in my group are older, settled in for life. I have nothing to fear from them. But what of all the other inmates I pass on my way in? Ms. Brown reads the panicked expressions on our faces. She says that the last time a volunteer was taken hostage was in the 1970s. But, she says, "every time you go inside you should say to yourself, 'I am now on the grounds of a prison,' and you should never, ever forget that."

Another almost two months go by before I can attend the final training session, this one held at OSP. There's a way to write about this session that begins like a joke. As there are so few things to laugh about in the world of mass incarceration, I'll begin it that way: *A rabbi, an imam, a born-again Christian, and a Mormon* (and me, and a law professor specializing in restorative justice—but these additions kind of ruin the setup) *walk into a bar.* Okay, it's a room. And I'm afraid that is both the beginning and the end of the joke. At the moment it strikes me as very funny that my co-volunteers-in-training are a rabbi, an imam, a born-again Christian, and a Mormon. But it is not surprising. The majority of the people who volunteer in prisons are religious folk, and the majority of programs brought into prisons are faith based.

The room we are all escorted to is on the second floor of the prison, a place you can get to without taking off shoes, removing jewelry, handing over your driver's license, getting your hand stamped, or anything. You just walk up these back stairs (accompanied) and you're there. It's amazing what a difference it makes to be treated like a normal person instead of a potential threat. There are six of us in the room, set up as a classroom with two-person tables facing the front. One side of the room is all windows, bringing in more natural light than anywhere else in the entire prison. At the front are two glass display cases, like you'd find in a museum. One of them features a collection of weapons fashioned by prisoners (and, obviously, confiscated): ingenious knives and shivs made from spoons and the guts of small electronics. The other case features jerry-rigged tattoo guns and screams *infection.* Also at the front is a pleasant, beefy ex-marine MP who is our trainer. He is refreshingly informal. As he puts up the first of roughly a zillion PowerPoint slides we'll be looking at during the next three hours, he tells us, laughing, "We have a policy for everything. Me, I learn by doing. If you learn by reading, this is your lucky day."

We spend the better part of an hour going through PREA slides. This is the initiative—with attending rules, regulations, and policies—that takes a hard stand against rape in prison. There was an online learning module about this, and Ms. Brown also presented a number of PREA slides, many of which are the same ones I'm looking at now. It is good to learn that the DOC takes sexual predators seriously, that the agency has declared a zero-tolerance policy for rape, that it has developed specific criteria for evaluating an inmate's vulnerability, and that it has codified and made public a process to investigate accusations and punish perpetrators. But of course that doesn't mean there are zero rapes in prison. I look at the slides and think of all the reasons a victim of rape in prison might not come forth, regardless of the promise of anonymity. Many are the same reasons so few women in the outside world press charges. But mostly I wonder why we volunteers are learning about this. This is not about inmates raping volunteers or volunteers raping inmates. Maybe it's about showing us what an ugly place prison can be. Or about making sure we understand how careful, thoughtful—and iron fisted—the DOC can be.

We turn from the prevalence of rape in prison to a depressing, far-reaching (and familiar) lecture on the many and varied ways prisoners can and do manipulate people like us, do-gooders from the outside. I heard this at the Dome training. I read it in one of the online modules. It's as if one of the main goals of these training sessions is to make you fearful of being anything but a hard-ass, to make you not just suspicious but on constant high alert.

"There are inmates who keep score on how many people they can compromise," says our trainer. "It's a game for them."

The message, again, is, Don't get overly familiar with inmates. I get it, really I do, and I now understand the mechanics of inmate manipulation. However, this not-getting-overly-familiar edict goes both ways, doesn't it? There is what they might know about me—about which I am already nervous but can do nothing about—but there is also what I might know about them. This could also put us on overly familiar terms, couldn't it? But here's the rub: The goal of the writing we do is self-discovery, and to do that is to unmask oneself. As I read the work the guys write, I am privy to their inner monologues, their emotional lives, the parts of themselves that they may have never shared before. Not everything they write is soul baring, but souls are being bared. How is this not personal? How do I maintain emotional distance as I read? And should I? The training says I should. My heart says I can't.

Seven

"DREAMS." THAT'S THE PROMPT I GIVE THEM TODAY. I'VE decided that rather than begin our sessions by launching into some lesson or discussion about writing, I should instead begin with a single-word prompt, a chance for them to write extemporaneously and freely. I am hoping that these five or ten minutes of writing set a mood in the room that my own words, my lesson, cannot. I am hoping to create an immediate and dramatic break between whatever they were doing and thinking about before they entered the room and what I'd like them to be thinking about now: stories and the power we have when we tell them. And, of course, I am hoping these free-form responses give me a window into their lives. It's seven thirty on a Saturday morning, the only time Steven could find for me on the activities schedule. I had to wake up at five and hit the freeway, not a great way to start to a weekend. But as the proposal for an official group winds its way through channels, and as I await my official ID badge, I have to seize every opportunity presented to me. I have to be dependable. And I have to be patient. Patience is a virtue. Just not one of mine.

We meet in our usual place, a big, bare, high-ceilinged room, an odd space to find in a place where everyone lives in six-by-eight cells. But this part of the prison was built close to a hundred years ago, and this floor, now the activities floor, used to be the chow hall. The room is windowless and empty except for one wooden table (made in the prison furniture shop) and some metal folding chairs. I see when I walk through the doorway that a new guy is sitting at the table. Steven told me that this guy, Lee, wanted to join the group. He praised Lee's intellect and his deep reading of philosophy. He said that Lee had been trying to get various writing projects going in the prison and saw this group as a way to help make that happen. Lee had apparently started a small, photocopied newsletter, *Tyro*, to publish prison writing, but it was a solo enterprise and got minimal response. He was more successful in putting together an anthology of writing from OSP inmates, compiled in a book that he made happen on a shoestring, without access to any of those tools that bring a modicum of polish and professionalism to amateur publishing. The book is unlovely and largely undistributed—Steven scrounged around and found me a copy—but it is nonetheless a triumph. To make it happen, in any form, is a triumph. I am happy to have Lee join. He is serving life without the possibility of parole. Only forty—a decade and a half younger than the next youngest man in the group—he has spent close to twenty of those forty years behind bars. His face, pale, unlined, looks like a boy's face. He sits almost motionless at the table, a study in self-containment.

Don isn't here this morning. The guys say they haven't seen him. Jimmie is still MIA. Eric comes in a little late, wound tight. His face seems thinner and more deeply lined than the last time I saw him. He tells us, his voice so quiet I have to strain to hear him, that he has a visitor coming later today, Tara, the girlfriend he hasn't seen in eleven years, the girlfriend who has just recently been released from her own term in prison. "You earned this visit, buddy," Jann says to him. Eric attempts but fails at a smile.

Jann focuses on eating an enormous apple fritter with one hand and writing with the other. Michael is distracted this morning. He starts to write, stops, gets up, leaves, comes back, sits down to write again. The guys can move freely from our room out to the even larger activities space where, this morning, there are a few coffee urns and boxes of donuts. I watch Michael, and it surprises me how easy it is to see him as he is now—an open, friendly, thoughtful, quick-with-a-little-joke-now-and-then, hefty-around-the-middle, middle-aged man—and not the man he was when he committed his crime, not a murderer. I thought that his ugly backstory would be the lens through which I saw him. And in a way it is, but not as I expected. I expected to feel fear, or anger, even revulsion. What I feel borders on respect. He took a life. He ruined his life. But he seems intent on remaking it.

"I'm just not all here," Michael says. He tells me that he is preparing for a rehabilitation panel hearing. It is many months away, but he is already consumed by it. Of course he is. His future may rest on this hearing. He puts his pencil down, shakes his head. He just can't concentrate. He apologizes.

Wil shifts uncomfortably in his chair and then gets up. "I can't do this prompt," he says, not so much to me but to the other men. "I can't write about my dreams. You wouldn't want to know what I dream about."

Wil has written about his crisis-companion work with inmates in the throes of psychotic episodes and PTSD panics. Maybe these encounters make their way into his dreams. I also know, from snippets gleaned, that Wil is an early-1960s Vietnam vet and that after his service he was hired as a private military contractor, a soldier of fortune—in other words, a mercenary—fighting for armies in Africa and the Middle East. I know that he has been in ninety-one firefights, three plane crashes, and thirty-four parachute jumps. I know that he's suffered five serious concussions, been shot and stabbed, and was declared dead three times. He told me all this, deadpan, as if reading items on a grocery list. He stands, tall and silent, as the other guys start to write. It's as if he is pausing for effect—certainly his silence has an effect—but I think maybe he is just considering if he wants to say anything more. Wil is a man of few words, which he carefully chooses.

"My dreams are too violent," he says. Then he walks out of the room to get another cup of coffee. Eric, Jann, and Lee continue to write.

Ten minutes in and they are still intent on the task. I give them another few minutes, then ask who wants to read. Miraculously, Lee volunteers. He reads in a quiet, accentless, slightly nasal voice. He dreams of being out on an ice shelf with the wind howling and the sea roiling fifty feet below. His dog, Colt, is his only companion. The dog falls into the sea. "I am alone. There is no one to help me save him. He will not last swimming against the waves in this Arctic Sea." Lee has his head down, reading. His lack of affect, as they say in psychological circles, is notable. I wonder if he sees that in the world of the dream, he is both the man on the ice shelf and the dog struggling to remain afloat. In the dream Lee considers throwing a rope down to try to save Colt. "But I have to go down there," he says, reading slowly. "That's the only way."

The room is silent, respectfully silent, for a long moment. Then Jann volunteers to go next, and it's a relief to listen to his dream. He dreams about growing a big vegetable garden and canning the harvest in rows of Mason jars. "I wake up thinking about food, and I go to sleep thinking about food," he says, laughing. The dream makes him happy. And hungry. He doesn't seem conscious of the planting, growing, harvesting metaphor, but he likes the dream. He likes the spaciousness of the garden landscape. He smiles as he reads what he's written. He is an engaging, almost theatrical speaker, the remaining legacy of his years in community theater. After reading about his dream, he launches, unbidden but perhaps sparked by all this talk of food, into a tale about "the Grill," the short-order takeout joint he ran out of his cell in the late 1980s. Yes, *a diner he ran from his prison cell, his maximum-security prison cell.*

—⁓—

The story of the Grill is a tale of astonishing ingenuity, extraordinary patience, and a clever craftiness that it is impossible not to admire. Just a few weeks ago, reading a book by a death row inmate, I had learned of that man's efforts to craft a mala—a string of prayer beads—despite that item being forbidden by prison authorities. He pulled a long thread from the seam of his prison jeans, sharpened a staple removed from a *Sports Illustrated* magazine, and used it to poke careful holes through Tylenol pills he had horded. Now Jann regales us with the details of his resourceful efforts. He tells us that he fashioned the cooktop for this operation from the metal seat attached to the cell wall, diligently sandpapering off decades of thick (probably lead-based) paint. The sandpaper was pilfered from the prison's furniture shop. He collected and then lashed together empty Bugler tobacco tins (smoking was permitted in those days), creating a fire pedestal under the seat/cooktop. Cooking power was provided by a series of tightly rolled toilet paper "donuts," each of which provided ninety seconds or so of intense heat. He created cooking utensils from the cigarette-rolling machine that came with Bugler tins. Ventilation was an issue—and after listening to Jann, I'm still not sure how he managed it, but it had something to do with the fact that A-block cells had solid doors not bars, a window that could partially open, and some fortunately positioned vent ducts.

Jann's Grill sold grilled cheese, ham and cheese, tuna melt, fried egg, and BLT sandwiches. The men on his cell block paid two packs of cigarettes for a meal. He could have charged three or four, he says. "But I wasn't greedy." He laughs a hearty laugh. He paid (in packs of cigarettes) fellow inmates in the bakery or dry stores to smuggle out his ingredients. It was a going concern, he says proudly, and it drove the guards crazy. He says this even more proudly. It's difficult to imagine how he got away with this, apparently for months and months. But it seems the stack of tiers and his venting system made it difficult to pinpoint where the inevitable (despite venting) cooking smells were coming from. Also all of his cooking equipment was easily disguised as something else. And, of course, the men in the block, especially the ones who frequented the Grill, had a vested interest in keeping the enterprise a secret. Not to mention the fact that Jann paid a couple of guys to "hold jigs" for him, prison slang for keeping an eye out.

We are all spellbound listening to Jann. I am the only one hearing about this for the first time, but Eric and Michael—even Lee with his I'm-not-giving-away-anything face—are clearly entertained. I think about how such enterprise and creativity would be rewarded in the free world. I wonder if Jann could have had an extraordinary future had he not murdered someone. And I think about how bizarre it seems that Jann is waxing nostalgic about the good old days when those good old days were in prison. But then I remember: His life is here. His memories are here. Jann has been down for thirty-four years.

—⁂—

We're back to dreams. It's Eric's turn. He was smiling a minute ago when Jann spun his yarn, but now he looks worried again, weight-of-the-world worried. He's still thinking about his visit with Tara. But he's written something, and he's ready to share it. "This is a dream I had just last night," he tells us. He was walking out in the prison yard when he saw a lone flower in bloom. He picked it and was immediately set on by a group of Russian prisoners who beat him and yelled at him to get off their turf. Again it's easy to see the metaphors here, the momentarily hopeful, then almost instantaneously frightening message of the dream. But it is also factual: There used to be flowers and trees in the yard—the guys say they remember those days—but a past warden had all landscaping removed. It obscured the vision from the sentry towers. And there is, indeed, a contingent of Russian prisoners in the prison.

"Russian mafia," Jann says. The guys nod. "After they finish their sentences here, they get deported," he explains for my benefit.

Wil has come back to the room in time to hear Eric's dream. He sits on the folding chair with his ramrod posture sipping bad coffee from a Styrofoam cup.

"Russians," he says. "My first kill was a Russian." We all look over at him. I can see that he is thinking about saying more. He doesn't.

Eight

THE CONVICTS' TEN COMMANDMENTS

(With Clarifications on the Golden Rule for Honest Johns)

Composed by a group of robbers at Leavenworth Federal Prison in 1947

   I   Thou shalt not bear witness against thy neighbor, false or otherwise.
Needs no clarification; Don't snitch!

   II   Thou shalt not steal from another con, nor from any working class person on the street.
Your fellow con is your peer and brother. You never take from family or friends. You rob only from the rich, not the poor.

   III   Thou shalt not disrespect thy fellow con in any way.
You never buck a line. When you do you are saying that everyone you crowded ahead of is a snitch or rapo and for that you could (and should) be killed. If you step on a con's foot or bump him, apologize or you could be killed.

   IV   Thou shalt not permit a stoolie or rapist to walk in thy presence or society, either in or out of prison.
Needs no clarification.

   V   Thou shalt not deviate from majority rule in any vote to strike or riot.
Cons are a unique society. They must hang together or they will hang separately.

   VI   Thou shalt not consider hypes, pimps, or dope dealers as convicts. They are inmates.
Hypes are weak to let dope control their lives, so the general feeling is, being weak they cannot be trusted. Pimps are not cons. They hide behind a whore's skirt to make a dollar by taking hers. Dope dealers contribute to the weakness of the weak and are a contributing factor in the destruction of children's lives. A CON IS A MAN!! He will never harm women and children.

   VII   Thou shalt not deny any and all assistance in any feasible escape plan of another con.

No con likes prison. So any who try to escape deserve any assistance you can give them.

VIII   Thou shalt not see nor move toward any act against prison rules so as to draw attention of staff.

If you look or move toward a fight, killing or escape, you draw staff attention (dry-snitching). There are only two reasons to look into another con's cell, to find something to steal or to snitch on. Doing so can cost you your life.

IX   Thou shalt not engage in any conversation with staff out of hearing of at least one solid con.

This gives witness you are not snitching.

X   Thou shalt not ask any favor of another con that you would not do freely for him, nor will you ever charge another con for any service you might be able to render.

You do not ask a brother to do what could lengthen his sentence unless you would do the same for him. You never charge for favors; you owe them. Pride prevents acceptance of any payment.

Michael hands me these ten commandments one afternoon in the form of a single rumpled sheet of loose-leaf paper covered in tightly packed cursive. The writing doesn't stop at the margins but goes to the very edge, the work of someone who had only one sheet of paper and much to write. "Honor among thieves" is a cliché, but clichés start somewhere and contain some truth.

He tells me these commandments, always handwritten, have been passed down, convict to convict, within OSP and from prison to prison, since they were first written seventy years ago. He doesn't know how long this particular piece of paper has been circulating, but it looks well used. We stand, side by side—but of course not touching—and read together.

"Convict is a term of respect, of honor," he tells me, as we begin reading. "When a convict calls someone an inmate, he is insulting him." He sees I'm confused. "You know, an *inmate*, like someone in a nut house." He further explains that a "hype" is—or was—prison slang for a needle user, a drug addict. "The convict code would be different today," he says, shaking his head. "So many guys are in here for drugs now. The culture has changed."

Not knowing that there was indeed a long-standing, iconic prison version of this, I had a few weeks back given the guys a "ten command-ments" prompt at the beginning of one of our sessions. After everyone wrote his list, and after what turned out to be a lively discussion about honor and respect among lifers, Michael mentioned the existence of this older list of "thou shalt nots." The others knew of it, but none had read it or at least remembered what they might have read. That makes it all the more interesting that so many of their commandments mirrored the ones written in the 1940s.

All the guys included some version of not snitching, not betraying confidences, not stealing, not lying, not cheating. Everyone referenced the need to respect—or not disrespect—fellow cons. Minding your own business was a popular theme, especially injunctions against "window shopping" (looking in someone else's cell). There were cautions about "fraternizing" with (variously) "the enemy," "the police," and "the pharaoh," which was separate from the issue of snitching and more an indication, I thought, of prisoners' antipathy toward the authorities who controlled them. Don included "Don't become friendly with female staff," which would not have been an issue in the 1940s.

"Thou shalt not count down your time aloud," was an interesting one. The men in the group, the ones who have the possibility of parole, who are calculating the years until their first, or second or third, chance at parole, are extremely sensitive to the fate of those who are serving life without that possibility. There's a kindness in that. A form of respect.

My favorite "thou shalt not" that came from one of the guys in the group—and was immediately and enthusiastically endorsed by the others—was "Thou shalt not forget the courtesy flush." That commandment, funny but in no way trivial to men who live together in cells the size of walk-in closets, cells with a bunk bed and a single exposed toilet, made me think hard. I thought not just about the gritty realities of incarcerated life and the small, hidden details of that life—I had thought about that, had been reading about that for a while now. I thought now about the act of making rules for yourself, how it is a liberating act, a defiant act, in a place where all the rules are made for you by others. I thought about how the flush commandment, all the commandments, were about recognizing, defining—even in a way celebrating—a separate community, a separate culture. And I thought about how similar the twenty-first-century men in my group were to the mid-twentieth-century men who first created the commandments—but also how different. Prison to those robbers and thieves was a wedge of time, an interval to be endured, an interruption to their real lives on the street. To the men in my group, prison *was* their life. The culture and community defined by the commandments was their *only* culture and community. It had been so for decades. It would be so for decades more—for some, until they died.

Nine

STEVEN MEETS ME AT THE FRONT DOOR TO THE PRISON. He takes the grammar book I want the guys to be able to use—I would need papal dispensation to bring it in myself—plus, after eyeing my spiral reporter's notebook, he grabs that too. (Those wires, who knows what use could be made of them?) I don't know what I'd do without him.

When I get up to the activities floor after the usual sign-in, ID check, metal scan, and three sets of clanging gates, I see that a Lifers' Club meeting is in progress. There are close to a hundred men sitting spread-legged on folding chairs, drinking coffee, and balancing donuts on brown paper towels on their thighs. They half listen as the president of the club fills them in on current projects and plans. I have to make my way through the auditorium-sized room to get to the smaller rooms in back, any one of which might be where the writers' group is slated to meet today. I skirt the chairs as best I can. But they are not set up in neat rows, or any rows, and there are no clear aisles on either side. So I have to weave my way through this sea of chairs, conscious that eyes, many eyes, follow me. I am not scared that one of these men—many of whom are prison elderly, some of whom are leaning on walkers, a few of whom sit in wheelchairs—will jump out and grab me. But I am deeply uncomfortable. The only woman. The only person in street clothes. Even my gait is different. Not just the gait of a woman but the surefooted, privileged stride of a free person. Ahead of me, just about to fold his lanky frame into a chair, is a guy I recognize. It's Dez, the man I met briefly more than a year ago when I first presented the writers' group idea to the prison education committee. I remember his quiet intensity, how carefully he chose his words, how melodic his voice was. At the time, he seemed interested in the group, but he has yet to show up for any of our sessions. Now he stands and acknowledges me with a crooked smile and a nod. We shake hands. We are being watched—not by the two guards behind the desk but by the guys sitting in the folding chairs. There is a subtext to what is happening. Dez, by acknowledging me, by extending his hand, has legitimized me in this room. I have instant credibility. Toward the back of the room, I see Michael, Don, and Lee. They are waiting to show me which room we've been assigned. Michael extends his big hand. Don offers me a wide smile. Lee almost makes eye contact.

I'm never sure who will show up for these sessions. I can't contact the men directly to remind them, so I depend on Steven to look ahead at the activities calendar and issue what are known as call passes for the men. A call pass allows a prisoner to be somewhere other than his cell, his work place, or the chow hall. Even if a man has a call pass, it doesn't mean he'll show up. I may never become accustomed to the fact that life within these walls can be simultaneously regimented and random, lockstep yet unpredictable. This afternoon Eric isn't here. The guys tell me he is work-ing overtime at the furniture factory. And Jann isn't here. He's injured, Michael says. He tells me that Jann has diabetes and has lost some feeling in his feet. Apparently he banged up his foot out in the yard, but didn't feel it, and now it is swollen and too painful for him to manage the long flight of stairs to the activities floor. But Wil is here, with his thousand-yard stare, and to my surprise, so is Jimmie. I haven't seen him in months. I take it as a good sign that he's decided to come back to the group.

—⁂—

I ask them what's going on, what's on their minds, and they begin to talk among themselves about the possibility that the relatively new president of the Lifers' Club might be stepping down. I've met Kyle, the new guy, only once, but my impression was that he took his leadership position seriously, that he was organized and worked hard. He is also a strong supporter of the writers' group. I'd hate to lose that. I interrupt to ask why Kyle is thinking of quitting.

"Too much drama," Michael says. He explains that Kyle is a "doer" who makes things happen and that someone thinks Kyle has too much influence and needs to be brought down a notch. So that "someone" is making things uncomfortable for Kyle. Or so the story goes. Prison is an "us versus them" culture. In this room the men serving time are the "us," and everyone who has control over them is "them." I don't know what the facts are, and probably they don't either. But the facts are beside the point.

"It's how this place works," Wil says. There's silence. I'm waiting for an explanation. I'm apparently the only one who doesn't get exactly what that means. "In here," says Wil, finally, "initiative isn't rewarded. It's feared, and it's punished." There is nothing more to be said.

The prompt I've decided on for today is a single word, "time." I've been thinking about the differences between *marking* time and *serving* time and *doing* time, about how time is experienced subjectively by all of us—and wondering how it is experienced by people whose time is rigidly controlled. People for whom time is a punishment.

—⁓—

They write for five minutes. Five heads (three of them bald: Michael, Don, Wil) bent over sheets of lined paper writing longhand, writing with intensity, writing nonstop. I let them write for another five minutes. I have the feeling that there is no time limit on how long they could write about time.

"I wish I could take a picture of all of you writing," I say when ten minutes are up. It's my signal for them to stop. "We are really the last generation to write by hand," I say.

Michael says he just learned how to use a computer six months ago. "My reality is 1989." He says he drives everyone nuts when he tries to use one of the computers on the activities floor to type up these assignments. "They see me sit down, and they find a reason to leave," he says, laughing.

I am reminded—I've lost count how many times I've now been reminded since I started learning from these men about life in prison— that the world I live in is dramatically different from the one they left behind when they "fell." Pokémon Go has been the big news for the past four days, so I tell them about it. None of them has ever used—or seen— a cell phone, let alone a smartphone. And only Wil, the ex-military guy, knows what GPS stands for. As I listen to myself attempt to explain the game to them, I hear how silly and superficial it sounds. I mean truly, laughably, shamefully silly and superficial. The world these men left behind, that all of us left behind, twenty, twenty-five, thirty years ago, seems more substantial by comparison, easier to make sense of, slower, calmer, somehow more solid. Time outside these walls has accelerated. I cannot fathom the culture shock they will experience if and when they get out.

I ask who would like to read first. Jimmie immediately volunteers.

"I no longer have time for the naysayers that tell me how wrong or misguided I am." His head is down, reading. "I no longer have time for people who tell me I can't, that I am wasting my time. That's just it, it's *my* time, and I have finally realized that when it's over I am the only one accountable for it." Jimmie's voice is quiet and measured, but there's a palpable intensity to it. He is clearly reading a personal manifesto. "This is my time," he says. "It's my life to make of it whatever I see fit."

I want to jump in and tell him how powerful that was, how writerly it was—he who has written that he is a "simple, uneducated man." But I am quiet. Jimmie hasn't finished. He's finished reading the piece, but he wants to say more.

"I've spent a lot of time . . . I've spent years doing things that I thought and others told me would get me in good with the parole board. I played that game. And then they denied me, and I realized that I could take my time back. That I was free to take my time back, to do what I wanted, not what I thought they wanted." He looks down at his sheet of paper. "I feel like my soul is free," he says.

I remember a dream Jimmie wrote about months ago, back when he was coming regularly to the group, back before his parole board hearing. In the dream Jimmie was released from prison, and once outside the gate, he was met by two women, Patty and Donna. Donna is the woman he married in prison. I'm not sure, and he didn't explain, who Patty is. In the dream Jimmie walks toward Donna, then falls to the ground, facedown, and is levitated. He told me at the time that he believed the dream was a premonition that the parole board was going to grant his release.

"Remember that release dream you wrote about, Jimmie?" I ask in the thoughtful silence that follows. He nods. "Well, I think you just now wrote about that. I think maybe that dream was not about your physical release from prison but about being released from expectations and obligations. It was about owning your own time." I hope I'm not overstepping my bounds. I'm not a dream analyst. I'm not a psychologist. But, really, can this be any clearer?

"Wow," Jimmie says. "I never thought of that. That could be it." Later, when he hands in his paper—I collect them so I can read them again and offer comments—I see that he has written in the margins in his nice, neat hand:

Do your own time! Time is running out!

My experience of feeling free in my spirit to do what I want could be an interpretation of my dream.

Michael's piece begins this way: "Which type of time are we talking about? The time on a clock, hours, minutes, seconds, or the kind of time I'm considered an expert at, that is, 'doing time.' I must admit I am getting pretty damn good at doing time. It is a better alternative to 'time doing you' or your time 'doing your people' . . ." He stops reading for a moment to explain to me. "There's this expression we have in prison," he says. "Don't make your family do your time." He means, he says, don't share your prison experience with your family, don't bring them in, don't make them see what kind of a life you're leading. "So I shut them out," he says. "I thought I was doing what was right for them, that I was leaving them alone, that I wasn't causing them more harm than I already had." Wil is nodding. "I thought it was selfish to share this with them, but I'm not sure I was right," Michael says. I ask him what he means.

"Well, I shut them out, so now I have nobody."

"Yeah," says Jimmie, "you just want to shut everything out." He talks about doing whatever he could to be transferred from a prison that was surrounded by a fence to this prison, which is surrounded by a twenty-five-foot concrete wall. "When I was at that other place, you could look out through the fence and see the world. I just couldn't handle that. Here you can't see anything."

"My cell window faces the wall of another cell block," says Wil. "I want it that way."

"How long since you've seen over the wall?" asks Michael. While Jimmie is thinking about that, Michael says, "For me it's been seven years."

"You can see over the wall from the windows of the library, can't you?" I ask. I have been in that room. I think it would be the most favorite space in the facility because of the expansive view over the wall and beyond the penitentiary grounds.

"When I go to the library, I purposely sit with my back to the window," Michael says. "I want to look, I really want to look, but I keep myself from turning around."

Wil's piece about time is about living in the moment, a classic Zen incantation. He is, it turns out, an ordained Zen Buddhist monk. As well as a guy serving two consecutive life without parole sentences. A trained mercenary and a yoga teacher. Like the unnamed man in the Kris Kristofferson song (which could apply to any of hundreds of guys in here), he's a "walking contradiction."

Lee's piece is, like every piece other than the dream prompt, intellectual not personal, something about time and space as relative but free will as an absolute. It sounds kind of Ayn Rand–ish to me. I make the mistake of saying that, and Lee balks. I don't know if Lee will ever open up and write about himself. The one piece he's shown me that is about the experience of incarceration—and not a well-informed minitreatise on philosophy, ethics, morality, and free will—is fiction. In the workshop, he doesn't often speak up. I get the feeling that he is elsewhere, always, and that place is a place of hurt.

We circle back to doing time. "We all do time in our own way," says Michael. "I thought I'd rather have death than life without parole, but Wil and Jimmie are showing me that there's a way to live here."

"You mean living a life of meaning?" I ask.

"Yeah," he says, looking over at Wil.

Wil's face is unreadable. But that doesn't stop me from trying to read it. He can pierce armor with that gimlet-eyed stare, but occasionally, just occasionally, there's a spark of warmth. The light flickers, then disappears. But I see it.

Ten

YOU'D THINK I WOULD BE USED TO IT BY NOW, THIS CHANGE
from outside to in, from free to caged. But today I am so flustered by the
rules and the guards and the sign-ins and the glare of the fluorescent
lights and the chatter of little kids who see their fathers only through
half-inch-thick polycarbonate that I turn the locker key the wrong way
and lose my quarter. It's the only money I've brought in with me. So I borrow a quarter from Steven, and I am so flustered that I place my driver's
license in the locker and turn the key. Until I get my official ID badge—
possibly the day before hell freezes over—I need my license to hand to
a guard to get my temporary visitor's badge. So I open the locker, grab
my license, borrow yet another quarter from Steven, and then slowly, as
if doing something *really* complicated for the first time, insert the coin
and turn the key ninety degrees to the left. And finally I get it right, this
little routine I have been doing now for close to a year.

It is a rocky start to this afternoon's session. I am already off-kilter
because it's been more than a month and a half since I've been at the
prison, one of the longest stretches away since I first started the group.
That month and a half has been spent in the most privileged way, on a
working vacation in Europe. I am very conscious that I am walking in
with a deep tan.

—⁂—

As Steven and I make our way upstairs to the activities floor, he apologizes. He forgot to issue call passes for the guys in the group. He's been
playing catch-up this morning, trying to get messages to the men, but he

says I shouldn't expect a good showing. "On the other hand," he says with a big smile, "I have a new guy for you." Steven takes pride in this group almost as much as I do, and he is happy, as I am, when word of mouth brings us another member.

The new guy is named James, Steven tells me, and he's young, younger even than Lee. James was tried and sentenced as a minor. He's already been in for twenty years, but he's only in his late thirties. Steven never reveals personal information he might have about any of the men, but he can tell me that James leads a small group of inmates who run almost monthly programs for at-risk high school kids. James was in high school when he committed his crime, when he killed someone. "So there's gonna be a new face up there," Steven says. "I hope you don't mind." I assure him that I don't. I wish the group would stabilize, both for my own pedagogical reasons and for a clear sense of group identity, but new members bring new energy and the chance for me to see prison life through another set of eyes. Also, with the unpredictable comings and goings of the men in the group, the sometimes hit-and-miss attendance, it's good to have more members, a few spares.

It's lucky that James is here because the call-pass blunder means only Michael and Lee have made it up to activities this afternoon. The sparse showing reminds me of the first halting days of the group, when three or four showed up, and I was lucky to have them. It also reminds me how far we've come since then. The group now has seven members: Michael, Don, Wil, Jimmie, Eric, Jann, and Lee. And James makes eight. That's a perfect number for a writing workshop.

I start by telling them about the books I've brought in for them. Because Steven preapproves a list I send him and then accompanies me through all the checkpoints and reviews and stamps the books, I'm allowed to bring in materials that can stay in the prison. ("If you bring it in, you take it out" was the rule I learned in training.) My book donations started with a request to bring in a (much-needed) grammar book, followed by my own book of essays about the challenges of writing. A trip up to the prison library showed me there was almost nothing there I could recommend as great narrative nonfiction, which is what I want them to learn how to write, so I started raiding my private library and combing the shelves of local used bookstores to find suitable books.

To write compelling prose, you should read compelling prose. To move from explaining and summarizing to telling stories, you should read work that does this. The collection started with extra copies I had of Steve Lopez's *The Soloist* and Jon Krakauer's *Into the Wild*. I thought the themes of independence, loss, and survival would resonate. I wanted them to read how to make a character come alive on the page. Today I bring in a few of my favorites: Tom Wolfe's *The Right Stuff*, Tony Horowitz's *Confederates in the Attic*, Jane Kramer's *The Last Cowboy*, and because I remember falling prey to its charms many years ago, Frank McCourt's *Angela's Ashes*. The idea is to create our own lending library with old-school sign-out cards. Michael has volunteered to be in charge of that. Steven says we can use a shelf in the Lifers' Club cage—I mean office—until he can come up with something better.

—◊—

After I've highlighted the books and given what I hope is a spirited minilecture on the importance of reading to writers, I start to tell them about today's five-minute writing prompt.

Michael interrupts. "Aren't you going to tell us about your trip?" he asks.

I hesitate. I try to figure out how to respond. I decide to say just what I'm thinking. They give me honesty. They deserve it in return.

"I wasn't going to talk about it," I say. "It feels funny, it feels bad, to talk about where I get to go when you're in here. I feel weird about it, like talking about a chocolate layer cake to a dieter."

Michael laughs. "No, no," he says, "we want to hear."

Lee is silent, but James says, "I'd love to hear about travels. It's as close as I can come to going anywhere."

Michael nods. "Tell us," he says.

So I offer them a stripped-down version without the tales of mountain hikes to ancient healing temples and fishing villages and hill towns. But I tell them something. I describe the narrow, winding streets and the lighthouse, the raki the locals drink that feels like it takes the enamel off your teeth as it burns a hole in your esophagus. They laugh. I make the transition back to our work by mentioning that while I was away I read Elena Ferrante's four-volume Neapolitan series. I don't expect they've ever heard of it or of her, but I tell them that a particular sentence in one of the books has been haunting me. And that sentence is today's prompt: "To write you have to want to have something survive you."

"What do you want to survive you?" I ask. "What do you want your legacy to be?" They put their heads down to write and immediately lose themselves in the activity, in their thoughts. As usual, they write long past the five-minute mark. As usual, I say five and give them ten.

—⁂—

Lee reads first. I am prepared for his usual high-minded treatise on individuality, self-reliance, honor, and virtue. And that's what he has written, but with a personal twist he rarely gives to his writing. His legacy, he writes, he hopes, will be to "make the world safe for people like me." He reads in his quiet, flat voice. People like him, he goes on to say, are people who do not follow the path of least resistance, who give their word and never break it, even to their own detriment. This must have something to do with his crime. He killed someone, I know. But he felt that was the right and honorable thing to do? He felt unapologetic about it? He could have copped some kind of plea or made life easier for himself, but he didn't? He gives hints of this in his writing, but I don't know the whole story. And these are questions you don't ask. You wait. When he is ready—if he is ever ready—I may find out.

James, the new guy, volunteers to read next. He sits in the rickety folding chair, straight and attentive, the first-day-of-class student, the eager student, the young student. I know James is thirty-eight, but he could easily pass for twenty-five. It's that gaze—there's something of the anxious little boy in it—and that smooth, wrinkle-free face, a face that hasn't seen much sun for two decades. What he reads is heartbreaking. What he wants to survive is the memory of "the me that was somebody's favorite," the kid who was loved by his family, the boy he was, the man he is no longer. He hopes that in writing honestly about himself, about his "regret and sorrow and search for forgiveness that I really feel unworthy of," he can regain a place in his family. Or at least a place in their memory. It is so hard to listen to this. I try to imagine what it must be like to feel this guilt, this shame. I cannot. There's nothing to say. I nod, and we are all silent for a moment.

Then it's Michael's turn. His response is simple and, like him, self-effacing. He isn't thinking about what he wants to survive him. He is thinking about right now, how writing about his own feelings and emotions, seeing them in print, helps him understand himself better. He "hopes like hell" what he writes does *not* survive him. He sees his own writing as "recycle bin" fodder.

I laugh. I tell him I disagree. "You write like you talk," I say. "It's relaxed and conversational, and that's a good thing."

"But?" he says.

It's extraordinary how eager these guys have been for criticism. When I praise their efforts, they are never entirely happy. "But," I say, "you could work on structure, on planning out what you want to say. You can talk it out first on paper and then really take a look at what you've got, where you want to go."

"Oh, you mean, like plot?" he says, half teasing. He knows what I mean. We've talked about plotting in class. I even had Steven find a whiteboard for me so I could illustrate plot. I used "The Three Little Pigs" as my example, to their delight and amusement. I wasn't being patronizing, and they knew it. I was just choosing a story I knew they all knew by heart, a story with a very clear plot line. Plus, it's good for them to remember that the wolf dies at the end.

The session is shorter today because the group is so small. As we're moving toward the door, James asks, haltingly, apologetically, if he can give me a story he's been working on. Then Steven, on our way together across the floor, hands me a two-pager from Wil. I read them both, sitting in my car in the OSP parking lot. Wil's story, a compact piece, a story boiled down to its essence, is about a man named Pup. Wil was Pup's crisis companion for three years. Pup recently died in the prison infirmary. "I sat with him, held his hand, hated cancer," Wil writes. His printing is so even, so precise that it looks like typewriting. His sentences are short, powerful, every word doing its job. Pup told Wil that he kept a "black box inside full of anger, hurt, and memories too horrible to think about." And that the box was locked. He's writing about Pup, but I'm sure he's writing about himself too. When he writes that "Pup hid his spirituality behind a convict posture, but kindness and empathy would escape," I know he is writing about himself, whether he knows it or not.

James's story is rough around the edges, but I can see the talent. He has written a prison story that transcends its environment, a story about the power of friendship and the masks we wear to seem tougher and less vulnerable. It's a story about the seventeen-year-old James on his way to prison and the tough-talking young woman he rides with in the transport van. Their friendship, through letters, is like that weed that somehow grows through the crack in a sidewalk. It shouldn't thrive. There's every reason for it not to thrive. It thrives. If the story ended there, it would be sweet and sappy. It doesn't end there, and it isn't sweet and sappy. It's sharp and smart and mournful. James has written—or is maybe three revisions away from having written—a wise and tragic story, a story I'd like to see published somewhere.

—⁂—

Two weeks later, I'm back at the prison. Steven is waiting for me, as he always does, at the front entrance. He takes my bag of preapproved books (John McPhee, Bill Bryson, Erik Larson, Anne Lamott). I thought about asking if I could bring in Ted Conover's *Newjack*—he goes undercover as a guard in Sing Sing—and Tom Wicker's extraordinary book about the Attica prison riot, *A Time to Die*, but I figured that would be pressing my luck. I ask about my official ID badge. It is going on four months—or is it now five?—since I completed all the training sessions. Steven shakes his head and tells me he's heard that the machine that makes the badges broke down.

Upstairs in our usual big, bare room, a surprise awaits: Dez, the man who stood up to shake my hand when I walked through the maze of chairs at the Lifers' Club meeting some months back, the man I met early on at the education advisory group. He is tall and long limbed with café au lait skin and styled dreadlocks, the neat coils and twists pulled back and secured at the crown of his head. I am not sure if seeing Dez here is a good surprise or a bad one. I love that new men are hearing about and coming to the group, and I know that Dez is a well-respected, high-visibility inmate, a leader. Steven has mentioned him. Michael, observing Dez stand to shake my hand at that Lifers' Club event, remarked on it, nodding his head in approval. I remember how impressed I was with Dez at the education meeting long ago, the intelligence of his comments, the sense that he was speaking from some deep place. But I also remember the chill, literally hair-raising, when I was told later the details of his crime. I didn't ask to know. And looking at him now, sitting barely five feet away, waiting to greet me, I wish I didn't.

In January 1994, Dez and a friend approached a young couple outside their apartment building and forced them at gunpoint into their car. Dez drove the car down the freeway, then off on a gravel road to a park along the river. They ordered the couple out of the car. Dez shot the guy in the head. His friend shot the woman three times and then pumped two more bullets into the guy. They left the bodies on the road. The two drove home in the murdered couple's car, met up with Dez's ex-girlfriend, and bragged to her about the killing. She didn't believe them, so they drove her back to the park to show her the two bodies. They pantomimed the murders during the reenactment. He was sixteen.

Twenty-two years later, he is a man who has grown up in prison and will die in prison.

I don't have time to process my feelings—I don't even know what my feelings *are* at the moment—because the guys are waiting for our session to begin. I look around the room to see who's here today. I was apparently so distracted by Dez's appearance that I failed to notice yet another new face in the circle of chairs. He introduces himself as Kaz. He seems to be a buddy of Michael's. It's hard to estimate anyone's age in prison, but Kaz is somewhere north of fifty. He has shoulder-length gray hair and a neatly trimmed Vandyke beard, and he wears rimless glasses. Out in the world beyond these walls, he could easily pass for a craft-beer maker or an aging hippie artisan. No one in the group, with the possible exception of Jimmie with his Irish-thug face, looks anything like the Hollywood version of a convict. It's fascinating how much we think we know. And wrong we are. Kaz has been at OSP for the past twelve years—that's just *this* stretch, he says, not exactly proudly but certainly, it seems to me, with an intent to establish himself among those who've served two, almost three times as long.

Don is here—I think he wins the attendance award—as are Michael, James, Lee, and Eric. No one knows where Jimmie is. They thought he was coming. Maybe he got a call pass to visiting, someone says. I hope so. I'd like to think of Jimmie sitting across from Donna right now. Once

again Jann is not here. The health concerns I had heard about, the com-
plications from his diabetes, are now, Michael tells me, part of a larger
meltdown that involves "legal and financial issues." Jann has now missed
more sessions than he's been to, and I should probably stop considering
him part of the group. If he shows up again, great, but I am not counting
on his return. I am counting—I do count—on Wil though: the stillness
of his presence; the challenge of his stare; his spare, wise, unsentimental
prose. Without his knowing it, or probably even wanting it, he gives the
group solidity. He anchors us. But Wil is not here today. It may be that
the guys know something, but they are not saying. I get the idea that his
absence may be health related.

Today our group of seven with two newcomers seems to work. I have
to remember that although Dez and Kaz are new to the group, they are
not strangers to the other men in the group. Lifers know each other. Men
who live in Alpha block know each other. When you live in such close
quarters for so many years, you know, or know of, just about everyone.
I am the only one who feels a bit off-kilter when someone new joins. But
I'm getting used to it. I hardly remember that Lee and James were newcomers just a short while ago.

I give them today's five-minute writing prompt, "hope." I've been
thinking a lot about hope these days, or rather the lack of it. I'm not sure
I know what hope means amid the extraordinary divisions in the world
outside these prison walls, in a country wallowing in nastiness and inci-
vility, at a time that seems full of fear and anger. What does hope mean
when you are spending your life in this other world, the one surrounded
by a twenty-five-foot-high concrete perimeter? Maybe I am looking for
a sense of hope from these guys. How strange is that?

Michael begins. He usually volunteers to go first. Today I volunteer
him, and he laughs. "I have a lot of hope," is how he begins his little essay.
"I have little of anything else, but more than my share of hope. If hope
paid by the pound, I'd be a wealthy man." What does he hold out hope
for? He hopes for his release. He hopes for knowledge. He hopes for the
Dallas Cowboys to win the Super Bowl. Next to him, Kaz, the new guy,
chuckles. Then Michael turns serious. He says he hopes for forgiveness,
not just from those he harmed but for the forgiveness he can give himself.
"I hope I come out of this a better man."

Kaz reads next. Because he just joined, he doesn't know that the idea is to be personal, to write from the heart. Instead he writes a statement about the nature of hope, that too much causes unrealistic expectations and too little leads to despair. It's good, clear thinking and good, clear writing but detached, like Lee's work. Lee follows suit, writing about hope in the abstract, hope giving us the power to act, the wherewithal to carry on. He is referring to his own sense of hope. I just wish he could write from that place. Eric, with his deeply furrowed brow—Eric, who looks like he worries enough for the whole world—writes that "hope is what helps me make it through another day in prison." He hopes to be successful, happy, loved, worthy, paroled, free, remembered. That's the order of his list. He ends with a statement about how hope isn't enough, that we have to work hard to fulfill our hope. Eric is working hard, so hard. He's got that parole date. He's got a chance, another one, his third one. He hopes he does not blow it. Don writes that hope is what you have when you're at the end of your rope, just hanging on, almost ready to let go. But you don't. Because something good might happen. To myself, I repeat: *Something good might happen.*

I am saddened as I listen to James's work. Although he is relatively new to the group, I have read quite a lot of his writing already. His story about Sophie, the girl he met in the transport van to prison, was really good. He's also given me other material he has been working on, perhaps for years. And so I feel I know him more than our short time together might suggest. I also know from Steven how much of a contribution James is making in prison with his Rise Up group for at-risk kids. James is young. He didn't come from the streets. He didn't come from a bad home. It seemed to me that he would be, of all of the men, the most full of hope. Not so.

"Hope is tough for me right now," he writes. His mother just died, and he can't imagine life without her. I know from writing he has given me how important his mother's love has been to him. She was the one who continued to support him, to accept him, to believe in him, even, as he has written in another essay, when he didn't believe in himself. "A prison sentence drains the word hope from my vocabulary." He has a quiet reading voice, like Lee's, and I have to strain to hear him. He goes on to list all the things he has going for him that had been leading him to believe he could be paroled in the not-too-distant future (which, in prison time, means maybe five years). He was a seventeen-year-old first-time offender. He has earned college degrees inside. He has fifteen years of clear conduct, the same industry job for the past thirteen years. He's held leadership positions in groups that help the prison community. But apparently he recently went through a mock parole hearing, and he writes, "My hope for parole diminished rapidly." The mock hearing program is pretty new in here and is supposed to help the guys prepare for the real thing. Former parole board members grill the prisoner. Other prisoners play the roles of victims or advocates. It is hard for me to understand how he—articulate, even tempered, clean-cut, earnest—would have gotten discouraging news from the mock parole board. I cannot imagine a more model prisoner.

Last is Dez. I've read a bit of his writing already, an autobiographical essay included in that anthology Lee worked on a few years ago. That is nothing like what he reads this afternoon. What he has written is lyrical, a prose poem. He writes with attention to sound and meter. His delivery is that of a street poet too, his cadence purposeful, his voice rising and falling. He begins: "Choosing hope / fuels spiritual fires / in cold chaos." Some of his lines are labored, but some slice right to the core: "I've witnessed human beings stripped of autonomy and humanity / And I have known them to still create beauty in hues of hope."

I realize, as I listen to him, that I am in the presence of a very different person than the man who, more than two decades ago, walked through the world with no moral compass. And I realize that I am also becoming different person too. Before I began to spend time here at this prison, in this room, with these men, before I read the stories that are offering me a window into their lives, I was not the kind of person who could sit and listen to Dez. I was not the kind of person who could look at him, really look at him. Or Michael, who stabbed his wife. Or Jimmie, who did Lord knows what. It is not my place to forgive any of these men for the terrible things they did, for the lives they ruined. But it is my place to think about forgiveness, to think about the possibility of change and the resurrection—yes, I think that's the word—of the soul.

Eleven

ALPHA BLOCK—THE HONOR BLOCK—IS WHERE ALMOST ALL of my guys live, everyone except Wil, who has given up that privilege to have a single-man cell in another block. A-block is the first destination on the tour Steven is giving me. As many times as I've been to OSP, I have seen only the waiting room, the control floor, the activities floor, the upstairs room used for trainings, and, twice, the library. A person can't wander. And getting a tour (unless one is a visiting dignitary or government official) is highly unlikely. It's not like there are docents at OSP. In general the people who run prisons would prefer to keep their business behind the walls that surround the place. It's not so much the desire to hide something bad (although, of course, it could be) but rather the ironfisted approach of the enterprise. It is all about control here. Preventing access is a form of control. It's how prisoners are controlled inside: no movement without a call pass, inmate badges scanned when entering and leaving a space. It's how visitors are controlled: certain hours, certain days, dress codes, metal scans, sign-ins, passes. It's how volunteers like me are controlled.

I have been borderline nagging Steven about a tour for months. I can't quite believe that he's made it happen, that we are here, standing side-by-side at the entrance to A-block. Steven reminds me that an inmate has to earn the privilege to live in A-block, which means level 3 status, a regular job, and a spotless conduct record for three years. Even then it may take years on a waiting list before a cot in a cell opens up. It's not that the cells themselves offer any luxury. They are roughly the same size as all the other cells, and, like most of the cells, house two men. There are the same barred iron doors across the front, the same harsh fluorescent lights bouncing off the concrete walls and walkways, and the same long line of cell after cell after cell stacked in tiers. Steven and I stand motionless for a long minute scanning the long row of cells, looking up to the second tier, watching two men play cards at a little metal table bolted to the floor in the central corridor. The scene looks like the set of every prison movie Hollywood ever made. In the blocks, it could be the 1940s or 1950s. Burt Lancaster could be gripping the steel bars of one of the cells. Broderick Crawford could be the warden.

That said, as the guys have already told me, A-block is not as bad as the others. The main part of A-block is only two tiers high—the other blocks are five tiers—so it feels, if such a word can be used in this context, more *intimate*, or at least slightly less numbingly institutional. Only 300 men live here compared with 560 in E-block, which means it's quieter. It's quieter also because of the kind of men who live here: well-behaved, determinedly prosocial men, careful men, men who will not yell or start fights or do anything that jeopardizes their place in honor block.

The big deal about A-block is that the men are free to leave their cells. Their cell doors are open all day. They can—with permission and call passes and restrictions—come and go. They can't wander. They can't be anywhere (the library, a classroom, the hobby shop) without permission, but they can be out in the wide hallway between the parallel row of tiers (there are a few tables out there) or in the small dayroom that has a TV and some exercise equipment. As level 3 inmates, they have more yard time than others, so they might be outside. But the most significant privilege of A-block, or so the guys in the writing group tell me, is that they have keys to their cells that fit little padlocks. The main guard-controlled levers keep the cell doors open all day, but the men can use padlocks to secure their "house" when they're away. This is a big deal. It means an inmate on honor block has a kind of ownership of his space, a small sense of control. In the rest of the prison, your cell door opens when an officer pulls a release lever for your row. That happens when it's time for chow or work or yard. Or when it's your assigned shower time. Otherwise, you're locked in.

We walk back onto the control floor, a big, bare, featureless space, maybe seventy-five by fifty feet, lined with portals to the cell blocks, the chow hall, the yard, and the shops that comprise the prison's industries. There's also an office for guards and a small windowed room with benches that everyone calls "the fishbowl." It's where, every day at five thirty in the morning and again at seven in the evening, inmates gather for "pill line" to be handed the prescription medications they take. The fishbowl, because it offers complete visibility, is also where a troublemaker might be sent awaiting some action on his fate. At one end of the control floor is the gated entrance, the one I come through after passing through all the checkpoints. At the other end, across a vast expanse of worn linoleum tile, is another gate that bars the concrete stairway to the second floor, the activities floor. Steven and I walk slowly across the control floor, poking our heads into the entryways to the other blocks. It is just the two of us moving through a small crowd of blue-jeaned men: black, white, Hispanic, Native, young, old; some swagger, some shuffle, a few hobble behind walkers, and one self-propels a wheelchair; ponytails, shaved heads, blued-out tattoos, biceps that strain the short sleeves of prison-issue blue T-shirts; some guys who look like you could bring them home to meet the folks; some guys you wouldn't want to meet in a dark alley. Or anywhere. It's lunchtime, and there's a lot of movement through the blocks, out into the control floor, and through the open doorway that leads to chow hall. Although I have occasionally seen female officers working here, right now I am the only woman within view. I follow Steven so closely that twice I step on his heels. But walking through the entryway that leads to the short outdoor passage to chow hall, I notice all of a sudden what a wide berth all the guys are giving me. When they see me, or when I come up alongside a knot of them, every man takes a big step away, a giant step. I think they may be even more conscious than I am about the possibility of our bodies accidentally touching—a swinging arm maybe, an unintended shoulder bump. In here they have much more to lose than I have to fear.

We stop to peek in the chow hall. It's big—maybe thirty by forty feet—windowless, institutional, loud. The air is thick with the smell of boiled hot dogs. The light is harsh and fluorescent. Just what you'd expect. The room, which seems low ceilinged because of its size, is dotted with dozens of four-person plastic tables bolted to the floor, with four bolted-down bench seats surrounding each table. As if there's not enough blue in here (the men all wear blue jeans and dark-blue shirts), the tables are blue. The men carry trays to their seats. They talk. There is an energy and liveliness to the room that belies its insistent drabness. This is a place inmates can socialize and, in the sense that this can happen at all behind bars, relax. Officers stand around the perimeter, watchful, arms crossed.

Out the door and straight ahead, we are in open territory—that is, ten acres that are encircled by the concrete walls. To the right is the yard, a big, grassy football-field-sized area surrounded by a running track. You could be looking at a high school athletic field if you ignored the two-and-a-half-story concrete wall looming in the near distance and chose to disregard the twenty-foot-high interior chain-link fence that separates the field from where Steven and I stand. In a few paces, Steven stops in front of another chain-link fence that cordons off a modest patch of grass. In the middle of the grassy patch is a concrete pad with a bronze plaque. On one side of the plaque is a replica of combat boots, on the other, a helmet. There are two stunted flagpoles, one flying the American flag, the other, a POW/MIA flag. It's a veterans' memorial. The Oregon Department of Veterans Affairs estimates that there are about 1,250 vets behind bars, 8.5 percent of the state's inmate population.

"The Vets' Club raised all the money themselves," Steven tells me. The cost, he says, was between $18,000 and $20,000.

Later, when I recount my tour to the guys in the writing group, Michael asks if I noticed how short the flagpoles were. I tell him I did.

"When they built it, the flags were flying high," he says. "But the guards in the tower complained that the flags were in their field of fire."

"Field of fire?"

"Yeah, if they wanted to shoot someone in the yard, the flags commemorating the veterans got in the way. So they lopped off the poles."

As Steven and I are looking at the memorial, a bulky, middle-aged inmate lumbers up to us and starts complaining about the metal crossbar on the fence that obscures a clear view of the memorial. "It'd be easy to move, ya know."

Steven nods, listens. He introduces the man as Frankie. We shake hands. His is big, rough, calloused. "Frankie is one of our gardeners," Steven says. Frankie ducks his head a little, nods. A few minutes later, as we are walking through the first of several outbuildings that house the various prison industries, Steven leans in—it is very noisy—and says, "That guy? The one by the vets' memorial? They call him Frankie Bangs." I wait for the explanation. "That's how he executed people—*bang, bang*," Steven says, watching for my reaction.

We're in the laundry now, passing from the "wet room" to the "dry room," walking past overflowing carts of towels and sheets, immense washing machines and dryers and folding machines, hundreds of men working. This is the second-largest commercial laundry in the state, Steven reminds me, and the prison's biggest employer. It is also the only one of the prison industries where a guy can work overtime if he wants to. Apparently the laundry took on so many contracts—hospitals, nursing homes, other institutions—that there's too much work to accomplish during regular hours. Although the jobs here are unskilled and repetitive, although the work conditions (at least in the room with the dryers) are ear-burstingly loud, jobs in the laundry industry are the most popular in the prison because of the overtime. Once a month, more or less, inmates on special work detail come in to vacuum the walls, the rafters, the floor, everywhere lint collects. Pounds of lint. Mountains of lint. It's awful work requiring face masks and earplugs. It pays five dollars for three hours of work and is considered a plum gig. James gets this assignment and is thrilled with the money.

Outside again, we walk by two nondescript one-story buildings that house other prison industries: the furniture manufacturing shop— "They make some really nice stuff in there," Steven says—and the metal fabrication shop.

"Metal fabrication?" I am incredulous. "I would think that would be a very bad idea in prison. Wouldn't this be a great place to, uh, make a shiv?"

Steven laughs. "Now you're thinking like a con," he says. "We've got metal detectors. Metal scanners. Everyone who works here gets scanned coming and going." He pauses, shakes his head. "You would not believe where some of these guys try to hide sharp objects." I can imagine. Steven decides my imagination needs help. "You know," he says, "up where the sun don't shine."

The call center is the next and last stop on the tour. It is the quietist, calmest, most sanitized of the prison industries: a big, dimly lit room illuminated by tiny blue lights, like a jazz club, with rows and rows of clear-sided cubicles. In each cubicle is an inmate on a telephone. The officer behind the big desk by the entry greets Steven warmly. I ask him what's going on, and after a fairly lengthy explanation, I still don't really know. It has something to do with selling some kind of a magazine or some corporate communications publication, I can't figure out exactly, but not really selling it, just getting a "yes, I'm interested" response so that someone else, someone not behind bars, follows up for the sale. Just like in real call centers, there's competition among the phone solicitors for the highest number of (in this case) yeses. On a whiteboard at the front of the room is a number representing the yes responses per shift or per week or per something. If the guys hit a certain number, which the officer says they will, something good happens, but I'm not sure what. I ask a few more questions, trying to understand the system, but I hear myself sounding impossibly dense, and I see that the officer in charge has lost interest in trying to explain this to me.

"The bottom line," he says, "is that they get good practice in communication skills."

I nod.

Don, who now works in the call center, once told me a story about a Hispanic guy who worked in the next cubicle over. Don listened as the guy joked around in Spanish to a nearby inmate and then switched to English—but a distinct brand of English, part Ebonics, part prison slang—to talk to another inmate. When it was time to work the phone, Don's cubicle neighbor switched again. Now his voice deepened, his speech slowed. He enunciated. He spoke virtually unaccented English. "If my eyes had been closed," Don told me, "I wouldn't have known it was the same guy." Certainly the call center offers ample opportunity to communicate with the outside world, even if it is only making what most of us would consider a junk call to read a script.

"The other thing about this job?" says the officer in charge with a laugh. "They learn how to take no for an answer."

Steven and I exchange a look. I'm not sure what he's thinking. What I'm thinking is this: *They need practice learning how to take no for an answer? No is what they get all day long.*

—⚏—

An hour later, upstairs on the activities floor, the men in the writers' group are sitting in high-school-style student desks arranged in a circle in the middle of the bare room. Today Don, Kaz, Michael, Wil, and Lee are here. Eric is out in the main room conducting an NA meeting. He's the president of that club and is working the steps with a seriousness of purpose, a ferocity that is formidable. James, I learn, is out in the laundry working overtime. He thinks that the more money he socks away, the better his chances of parole. He might be right. Showing industriousness, dependability, and the ability to save rather than spend all count for something. Jann is MIA. I have decided to just stop expecting that he will ever return. Jimmie is missing, which is not unusual. More troubling is Dez's absence. Despite his brief time in the group, he has become an indispensable member. He is an already talented writer who is a pleasure to edit, and he is an eager learner. I don't want to lose him.

We're talking about the groups' first official publication, a little in-house newsletter that is going to feature short essays by seven of the men. The essays began as one of the five-minute prompts. The word of the day was "trust," and the responses were so varied and so powerful that I wanted the men to be able to spend more time thinking through and bringing clarity to their thoughts. Michael had written that he no longer trusted anyone. Kaz wrote that trust was a "luxury" he could not afford. Jimmie wrote about growing up in a household of "deeply dysfunctional" people—"Many of those I loved would be incarcerated today"—where he never learned to trust. But then there was Dez, who proclaimed that "the trustworthiest people I know are prisoners." Since that first brief exercise, the small essays have been edited several times by me, honed by the authors, read by everyone in the group, and they are now ready to go. I thought the project would give us a collaborative goal and also give the guys a sense that what they are writing is worthwhile, worth seeing in print—even if the "in print" is just a few photocopied pages. Lee, with his access to a computer and permission to use the photocopy machine in the activities office, is the guy in charge of making it happen. We have a spiffy logo for the newsletter courtesy of pro bono work by a talented graphic artist who is a friend and now happens to be my daughter-in-law.

The publication has no distribution. That would be a whole separate set of permissions, a level of administrative review that seems overblown for this humble effort. And quite possibly could take months. And quite possibly could result in no. So the newsletter is an under-the-radar operation just meant for the men in the group. But I love that it is something they can each hold in their hands, that contains work they have sweat over, edited, and revised, that the others in the group contributed to the editing process. In a place where accomplishments can be few and far between, this *is* an accomplishment. They seem genuinely pleased with themselves. The experience has spurred my own thinking: What other avenues are available for the publication of their work? How can I help them move their stories, the best of their stories, beyond these walls?

After the newsletter plans are set, I give them today's prompt, "determination." They set to work as usual, shoulders hunched, foreheads furrowed, pencils scratching on lined paper. I am still thrilled by the sight. A minute into the prompt, Dez walks in, long strides, head down.

"Better late than never," I say. I mean it lightheartedly, but when he looks up and I see his somber face, I regret it instantly. "I'm glad you're here," I say. Which is what I should have said the first time. As he folds his lanky frame into the student desk, I give him the prompt. He starts in immediately.

Dez's riff on "determination" chronicles what happened during the last half hour as he tried to make it up to activities to get to the group. First he's held up in a meeting with "three supervisors who have seven different ideas about two projects" and can't agree. Already late, he rushes to the control floor to make his way up to activities, but an officer "with ambition" tells him he has to wait for the line to be called. (That's a scheduled lineup of all the men who need to be somewhere. They are processed en masse.) Dez tells the officer he's already twenty minutes late. "Go away," the guard tells him. "Come back for the line. Five minutes." Ten minutes later, the line starts to move. But Dez realizes he's forgotten his ID. He goes back across control to get the badge from his cell. It's on a lanyard that should be around his neck at all times. Now he can't find his call pass, his written permission to be up on activities for the writing group. Searches for it. Finds it. Goes back to control. Shows documents. Gets through. Here's how he ends his piece:

> Never once did my pace slow nor my stride stumble . . .
> Unmanaged managers, inaccurate clocks, officers asserting new authority
>   could not
> deter me in the least.
> I was gonna make it.

Now *that* is determination. That is the living definition of determination. It is also, despite the purportedly beneficial learn-how-to-take-no-for-an-answer lessons of the call center, a lesson in how to persist in the face of challenges and circumstances, how not to be discouraged, how not to take no for an answer.

Twelve

WE'RE MEETING TODAY DOWNSTAIRS IN THE VISITORS' ROOM.
It is here families come to see their incarcerated relatives during permissible hours. It is a big, gray, windowless space that is so insistently institutional and aggressively unwelcoming that it must have been thoughtfully designed this way. We've been moved here because the entire second floor—the big auditorium space and the smaller rooms like the ones we use for the writers' group—is temporarily closed to all activities. That's because the floor of the big room is littered with overstuffed black plastic garbage bags filled with the possessions of scores of inmates awaiting transfers to other prisons. They were some of the men involved in the fight—let's call it a riot—last week.

More than 150 inmates fought and skirmished with each other from Friday afternoon through Saturday morning. Staff used chemical spray to control the situation and break up the fights. Multiple inmates were, according to the guys, "thrown in the hole" and, according to the DOC spokesperson, "escorted to restrictive housing." The media, quoting the tight-lipped DOC spokesperson, reported no staff injuries or *serious* inmate injuries. During the fight itself and for four days afterward, the place was on total lockdown. Total lockdown means no one leaves his cell—not for meals or showers or infirmary call, and of course not for phone calls, visits, yard, activities, clubs. There are two exceptions to this: the culinary workers who report directly to the kitchen (they make the sack meals that are delivered to the cells) and, interestingly, a scaled-down crew of men who work in the prison's laundry operation. As a prime moneymaker for the Department of Corrections, it cannot shut down. Otherwise, everyone is cell bound for twenty-four hours day. You'd think this would be crazy-making for the inmates, but several of my guys say they don't really mind it.

"Kind of a vacation," Michael says.

"No drama," Lee adds.

DOC authorities didn't say if the fights were gang related, but my guys tell me it was whites versus Hispanics and that the fight "came in with them," meaning these were blood feuds from the outside just awaiting an opportunity to surface inside. Once order was restored, it was decided to ship out the troublemakers to other prisons in the state. If they stayed at OSP, it would be just a matter of time before the next fight erupted. Lockdown is now over, but until those declared trouble-makers are processed out, along with their garbage bags of belongings, there's no access for anyone to any of the activity spaces up on the second floor.

I'm thankful the group session wasn't cancelled because we lost our space. I'm sure Steven was behind that. I appreciate more and more the part he is playing in the continuation and, I would say, success of the group. Mostly his efforts are low key and behind the scenes, smoothing out rough edges, writing an email to just the right person at just the right time, waiting when waiting is strategic. He is my fairy godfather. I think about the intermittent, stumbling way I was proceeding before I met Steven. I think about how one person, without hoopla, without fuss or ego, can make such an enormous difference.

His influence goes beyond the writing group. He is the Little Engine That Could for a number of the prison's activities programs. Overseeing activities and clubs is his job, sure, but he doesn't have to perform it with such enthusiasm. He doesn't have to look for ways to help, to innovate, to create experiences and opportunities. Others in his position might look for ways to say no. He looks for ways to say yes. I think it's because he believes in the guys. And he believes in them not because he's a bleeding-heart liberal (remember: he's a motorcycle-riding navy vet with Tea Party tendencies), not because he's a Rousseauian innate-goodness-of-man kind of guy (he's seen too much for that), but because he has a deep—enviably deep—well of optimism. Optimism is not seeing the world through rose-colored glasses. Optimism is seeing the world how it is—as in, sometimes the glass really is half empty or completely empty—but believing you can do something about it. You can replenish the water in that glass. That's what Steven is doing, pouring water in the glass, with my writers' group, with a music group he is trying to get off the ground, with the other groups he is in charge of.

So here we are in the visitors' room trying to find a little corner where we can conduct our session. The room is packed with members of the Lifers' Club. That meeting had been scheduled for the auditorium space on the activities floor. But, like us, they can't meet upstairs either. There may be as many as sixty men here finding places to sit on the vinyl couches and chairs. They're not here for the program (there isn't much of one) but rather for the donuts. Or this is what Michael tells me, as he grabs two for himself and offers to bring me one. He motions me to an unoccupied corner near the back of the room where he and Don help me arrange chairs in a tight circle. It's just Michael, Don, Lee, and James today. With the confusion of lockdown, the change of venue, and the staff's attention to getting things back to normal, it's no surprise that everyone in the group didn't get a call pass. Or it may be that after the multiday lockdown, they have other things to attend to. I'm astonished *anyone* is here. And more than a little pleased.

Just as we settle in, another guy swaggers over, and I mean swaggers. He looks like central casting sent him in response to a "please send over a hardened criminal" call. He's the kind of muscular you get from working out on the weight pile in the yard every day—all pecs, traps, and delts. His full-sleeve arm tattoos are blue and blurry. Classic prison tatts. The ink was probably either taken from a ballpoint pen or concocted by mixing melted plastic, soot, and shampoo. The tattooing device was undoubtedly fashioned out of some combination of mechanical pencil parts, a magnet, a radio transistor, staples, paperclips, and guitar strings.

Yes, I know this.

Sterilization of equipment is, of course, not possible. What is possible is transmission of hepatitis and HIV. Tattoo equipment is considered contraband—its possession is punishable (Rules of Misconduct 1.20 "Possession of Body Modification Paraphernalia")—and the act itself is considered a punishable form of self-mutilation (Rules of Misconduct 2.45). That's why having so many tattoos is so undeniably, inarguably, visibly badass. The guy's neck is completely inked. He's also got a series of little diamond shapes tattooed under both eyes. That must have hurt.

The eyes are stop-dead-in-your-tracks cold.

He wants to join the group.

Technically, the group is open to any lifer. This guy—Shawn is his name—is a lifer, and he does not look like a person one wants to say no to. At least, I'm not going to say no. I explain that it's a writers' group, that we've been meeting for quite a while, that we write both during the session and after. I use the word "homework," thinking this might be a deterrent.

He nods. "I'm all about it," he says.

Don gets up to find another chair for Shawn. He places it—and this has to be on purpose—a few inches back from the five chairs the rest of us inhabit that we've arranged in a circle. Shawn sits. He sits with his legs spread far apart in that I'm-taking-up-as-much-room-as-I-can aggressive male stance that every woman knows. But Shawn's legs are spread so very far apart, almost 180 degrees, that the message is beyond that: antagonistic, belligerent, almost taunting. Yes, cocky. Yes, a purposeful pun. On the other hand, for an instant, I marvel at the dancer-like opening of his hip flexors.

The session this afternoon is pretty much a bust. I have them write on "forgiveness," but it is almost impossible for anyone to concentrate enough to write because of the noise level in the visitors' room. Sounds ricochet off the bare concrete walls, and with sixty or seventy people in here, there is a lot of sound. When it's time to take turns reading aloud, it's almost impossible to hear what anyone has written. It's not just the din of the Lifers' Club members talking trash, joking, making the most of human interaction after the multiday lockdown. It's the interminable club announcements made via scratchy handheld mic; the very visible presence of officers stationed around the room, standing with arms folded across their chests, scanning the crowd; the whole pent-up, post-lockdown mood of the place.

Plus, I am unnerved by the new guy.

"Unnerved" is a euphemism.

We must end early, after only an hour, and I'm fine with that. The guys cue up behind the crowd of donut-eating lifers. I wait until the room empties and follow Steven out the door, down the corridor, past the first guard station, through the gates. At the second guard station, I insert my right hand with its ultraviolet-ink stamp through the slot, surrender my visitor badge, and reclaim my driver's license.

Steven waits patiently. "That new guy . . ." he says, his voice trailing off. Of course he noticed him. "Is he wanting to join the group?" We walk up the final long corridor together, side by side. I shoot him a pleading look.

"I hope not," I say.

He nods. He's got my back.

Thirteen

WHEN I ARRIVE ON THE ACTIVITIES FLOOR THIS AFTERNOON, I see Wil leading his yoga class, seventeen guys on mats doing down dogs and cat cows. They are set up on the left side of the cavernous multi-purpose room in front of the cages that house the prisons' clubs. I walk as close to the class as I can without being obvious and listen for a moment as Wil instructs—military style, not the "open your heart and breath into that space" kind of cueing you expect from your yoga instructor. I watch the men, gray-haired, balding, in their baggy prison jeans and blue T-shirts, hold forearm planks.

I make my way over to our room, stopping at the threshold to check out who's there. Lee, Don, Kaz, Michael, James, and Dez are sitting around the big built-in-the-prison conference table. I do not see Shawn, the spread-legged, tattooed-neck guy who joined in the last session and said he'd be back. I don't realize I am holding my breath until I hear myself exhale, apparently with some force. Don turns his head, gets up, walks over to ask me if I'm okay. "Very okay," I say. Later when I ask Steven about Shawn joining the group, he smiles, shaking his head. "That just ain't gonna happen," he responds.

Wil finishes leading his class and comes in a few minutes late. I ask him about the class. I knew he taught yoga, but I'd never seen it in action. He says a chronic care nurse in the infirmary asked him to lead it years ago. It's called "medical yoga," he says.

"You mean 'Yoga for Old Men,'" quips Michael. Michael is sporting a new look: moustache, Vandyke beard, soul patch. His bald head gleams under the fluorescent lights. He looks like a WWF superstar gone to seed.

Wil gives him the kind of look only Wil can give: steely-eyed, taking his measure, showing no mercy. A Clint-Eastwood-tough-old-man-don't-fuck-with-me look. He lets that look settle in for at least two beats longer than it has to. Eastwood staring into the camera. Then his eyes narrow and crinkle up at the edges. This is Wil's version of a smile. It turns out he's playing with Michael.

"You see," he says, addressing us all but nodding at Michael, "I get no respect." Deadpan sarcasm. Wil is the most respected man at the table, one of the most respected lifers. And now he's on a roll.

"You hurt my feelings," Wil says. He is being jocular. Deadpan jocular. I've known Wil for more than a year, and I've never seen him like this. Maybe this is what he is really like, but he wasn't allowing me to see it? Maybe he's high on yoga. "Yep, you hurt my feelings," he repeats.

"Oh, we hurt *both* your feelings?" counters Kaz. Kaz takes his writing seriously but not himself. Kind of like Michael. In fact, I am beginning to think of Kaz as Michael's sidekick.

There is this second of silence while everyone in the room decides if the bantering has gone too far. The decision: it hasn't. Wil almost smiles. Michael guffaws and fist-bumps Kaz. Lee looks up, moderately amused. I, without thinking, forgetting for a moment where I am and the hours of training I've been through and what I am and am not supposed to do, reach out and ever so lightly poke my elbow into Wil's forearm. He crinkles his eyes at me.

Is it too weird to say that a protosmile from a near octogenarian serving two consecutive life without parole sentences for aggravated murder warms my heart? I'll say it anyway.

—⁓—

I'd been puzzling over the prompt for today and decided at the last moment, in the car in the OSP parking lot, to use "I believe . . ." What *do* they believe, these men who've spent most of their adult lives in prison? I am invariably surprised by what they write in response to my prompts. I am, time and again, struck by their intelligence, their insight, their candor, their humor. The fact that I am so surprised says just as much about me and the stereotypes I have about people who commit crimes as it does about them and the way they have changed over their long years of incarceration.

Wil starts us off with a series of bold assertions: "I believe in the necessity of change. I believe middle ground evolves from conflicting belief systems. I believe in belonging. I believe in responsibility to the past." I wonder how many of us would be capable of stating our core beliefs so succinctly—and with less than five minutes to think about it.

Michael writes an unusually thoughtful paragraph that begins, "I believe that the few need to step up and voice the truth for the many who are too worried or scared to speak." He could be channeling Nelson Mandela. But more than politics, this is a declaration of the power of speech, the power of words. That's what we're about here in this room.

Lee, no surprise, takes the philosophical high road. "I believe that history is not over," he says, reading quietly from his paper. Lee, who dropped out of school when he was fourteen and has been in prison since he was eighteen, writes about Francis Fukuyama's provocative 1989 essay that proclaimed the end of mankind's ideological evolution and the universalization of Western liberal democracy as the final form of human government. And, yes, I looked it up when I got home. Because I, who have been to college (three of them in fact), *had* to look it up. And, informative *Wikipedia* entry notwithstanding, I don't get it.

Kaz writes that he believes "there's a reason for it all," pausing for a beat before he adds, "although this reason has yet to manifest itself to me." Which gets a laugh.

Don follows with random "I believe" statements, a playful take on the prompt: He believes the earth is round. He believes in Christmas but not Santa Claus. He believes "the color of teal blue is a mystical memory of someone's eyes." My heart clenches at that one.

Before he starts to read, Dez announces that he no longer wants to be called Dez. "That was my street name," he says. "That's not who I am." Henceforth, he asks us all to call him his given name, Sterling. Sterling tilts back in his chair and reads: "I believe I recently fell in love." This gets everyone's attention. "The first thought on my mind when I awake is the beloved," he continues, holding us, then spinning it out for three more lyrically opaque sentences until this, which he recites as poetry: "Yes / I believe I have fallen in love / with my breath." Wil, Mr. Yoga, closes his eyes for a moment. I love the mix of these responses, the way Lee's studied intellectualism is countered by Don's lightheartedness, how Kaz delivers a punch line and Dez—I mean, Sterling—writes poetry.

James is the last to read and the hardest to listen to. Just as he was walking into the room this afternoon, Steven handed him a notice that, I find out later, amounts to the gutting of a project James has been working on all year, the outreach program that targets at-risk teens. Creating and fostering this program has given James's prison life a purpose. The program was launched and seemed to be going well, but it caught the attention of someone within the vast bureaucracy that is the Department of Corrections, and apparently there are liability issues or other legal issues that will now prevent actual at-risk kids from being involved. Well-behaved teens, the ones who least need the program, will apparently still be welcomed.

Through the first half hour of our session today, the exchanging of pleasantries and small talk that creates the separation between their lives outside this room and our time together, James has been silent. He has been staring at the papers Steven gave him, reading, rereading, head down. When I gave the prompt, he made a visible effort to come back from wherever he was. He turned the stack of papers upside down next to him and started writing. Now it is his turn to read. He looks at me. His eyes are red. "You don't want to hear what I've written," he says.

"You don't have to read aloud, James," I say. "It's always a choice."

I watch his face. To be given a choice is gift. I can see his shoulders rise and fall as he takes a deep breath. Then he looks down at his paper and reads in an almost inaudible voice: "I believe good effort is pointless. I believe that at some point even a rose that grows through the cracks of concrete withers and fades when the search for sunlight is overshadowed by unrelenting poor weather."

There is nothing to say. But I have to say something. "Did it help at all to write that out, James?" I ask.

He pauses for what seems like a long time. Finally he says in a choked voice, "A little." I can't tell if that's what he feels or if that's what he knows I want to hear. Maybe both.

—∞—

What James wrote, the conversion of his sorrow into words and the emotion behind that, focuses my attention for the next several days. I want to find publishing opportunities for the men beyond our modest little newsletter. I want to help get their work out into the world. It's not just that I think they have important stories to tell, stories the rest of us could benefit from hearing. It is also that the alchemy of changing experience into story can be life altering. For some of the men, not all of them of course, but some, it may have been the inability to use words to express what they felt that got them where they are now. I wonder, if Michael could have talked about his marriage, his unquestioned notions of what his "manly" role was, his anger, would that relationship have devolved into abuse . . . and murder? If Jimmie could have seen his violent and abusive family as the plot of a story he had the power to rewrite, would things have turned out as they did? If Wil had been exposed to the power of words instead of the power of guns and ammo, would he have made other choices? Does this sound absurdly naive? Yes. But doesn't it also sound hopeful?

My research into publishing opportunities turns up the PEN America Prison Writing Contest, an annual national competition for nonfiction, fiction, poetry, and drama open only to prisoners. PEN America is a big deal, a champion of the freedom to write, an organization dedicated to, in its own words, "recognizing the power of the word to transform the world." The contest offers cash prizes, not an insignificant factor for men whose monthly take-home salary for full-time work can be less than a hundred dollars. But to my mind the prize money is nothing compared to the public recognition and respect their work would get should one of their submissions be chosen. I know that's a big *should*. Many thousands of inmates from prisons and jails all across the country send in submissions every year. I study the PEN website carefully, reading the first-, second-, and third-place winners in essays and memoir. They're good, but I think the writing of at least a few of the men in my group could be competitive. The deadline for submissions is a very long way away, close to a year, so we've got time to choose just the right story and work through as many revisions as it takes. Having a lofty goal is good. And having a longer piece we can spend time on could be a terrific way to elevate their writing to the next level. It doesn't escape my thinking that recognition, should it come, would reflect well on the group as a whole, on Steven for his part in making the group happen, and even on the OSP administrators who, at various points, gave their okays. But I am getting way ahead of myself. First I have to see what the guys think.

When I come in two weeks later, I bring with me two thick packets of photocopied first-, second-, and third-prize PEN winners of the past three years. Without preamble, I read excerpts from a paragraph from one of the stories. It's about the writer's experience during lockdowns:

> We used to cook meals in our hot pots and hand booze back and forth in the middle of the night. I had been through the 14-day lockdown when the old bruiser stomped that kid into a puddle. I had withstood a couple during the hottest weeks of summer. I'd had them . . . when they brought dogs through, leaving paw prints on my blankets. I'd been in them during holidays and during prison softball championships. I was locked down on my 32nd birthday and had a card signed by all of my friends, sent down the tier one cell at a time.

"The guy who wrote that . . ." I say, my voice trailing off. "He's at a max prison in Minnesota." The men have been nodding as they listen. They are all too familiar with lockdowns. "You might like to know that he got two hundred dollars in prize money for the story." Now that I have their attention, I launch into a description of the contest, of PEN America and its worldwide reputation, of how I think we should work on submissions for the next contest. It's a tougher sell than I thought.

"Writing about prison is boring to me," says Don.

"But people don't know who we are and how we live," counters Eric, bless him.

"Yeah," says Jimmie, "it's because they don't wanna know."

"Right," says Michael.

"If I do this, if I write, I'm not gonna write the same old story," Jimmie says. "I want to write about the underside." I thought prison was *already* the underside. I ask him what he means. I can see he's already thinking his way into an idea even if he doesn't realize it. That's a good thing. "I'd write about the hypocrisy in here, about how so many people are pretending, how so many people are just spending their time gaming the system." I ask them to think about it, to read a few of the pieces in the packets I'll leave with them. We have plenty of time.

"I don't need to think about it," says Sterling (Dez). "I'm there." He says he'll bring in something for me to look at next time. He could be the spark that ignites this.

—⁂—

"Joy" is today's prompt. This is what I feel as I watch them, intent on their writing. Five minutes go by. I give them another five. Then another two or three after that. I am not writing along with them—as they expressly want me to do—out of a now-familiar combination of guilt (I have so much joy in my life; they have so little) and reticence (how much do I want them to know about my life anyway?). But I have brought in a short piece I wrote for my blog a while back about the surprise joy of small, spontaneous moments. No big, grand, look-at-all-the-joy-in-my-life statement. Just a few sentences about watching my cat slink along the top rail of a fence. This seems like a safe bet. But maybe not. It's impossible to mask my privilege. I just try to tone it down.

Jimmie is the first to share. "There is no joy in incarceration," he writes. This is what I expected to hear. But then he calls bullshit on that. He writes that he does find "plenty of good times"—which I guess is how he has redefined "joy"—as long as he keeps his expectations low and his vision myopic. He enjoys his work as a clerk in the metal shop. He laughs with his coworkers. These are his good times.

Michael also redefines joy, "a word I haven't used or thought about in quite some time." Real joy would be freedom, which is "only a dream somewhere in the distant future." His joy right now is, like Jimmie's, constrained by his circumstances. His greatest delight? Watching college football on Saturday mornings on the little TV set in his cell.

Don takes the opposite approach. He doesn't write about prison, about whether he finds moments of pleasure or enjoyment in the life he has been living inside these walls. Instead he imagines the joy of popping open a can of beer at a picnic, of feeling the wind in his face while driving a convertible. These memories are thirty-three years old. What strikes me is how alive these moments are for him still, what specificity he brings to the writing of these little scenes, how delicately and wistfully he captures them. I think about the discussion in the group a while ago when Michael said he couldn't bear to look out the windows of the prison's library. You can see over the wall from those windows. And for Michael it was too painful to see outside, to be reminded of all the life taking place outside. There are as many ways of dealing with decades—with a lifetime—of incarceration as there are people trying to live those lives. Don keeps the memory of his previous life alive. Michael needs to shut the door. Lee buries himself in philosophy. Sterling writes and writes and in the process transforms himself from punk to poet. James is a workaholic. Eric is a worrier. Jimmie learns the hard way because his life has always been the hard way. Wil? I don't know. Sometimes he's the soldier so comfortable with routine and restriction that prison doesn't offer any challenges. But then other times he's the yogi, immersed only in the moment.

Eric reads next. He is also looking outside for joy, but his vision, unlike Don's, is for the future. That's because Eric *has* a future. He has a parole date. This is—or will be—a joyful event. But for Eric, his happiness seems almost immediately overshadowed by his worry. He has been paroled before. He has returned. Can he make it this time? Can he stay clean? The need to keep strengthening that resolve, to keep talking the talk, is why Eric goes to NA meetings instead of writers' group meetings when the two conflict. Now, writing about joy in the future, he refers only elliptically to his release. To do so otherwise would be disrespectful to the other men. He imagines the joy when his daughter is able to say she loves him again. "The greatest joy," he writes, "is now there is a chance."

Then Lee, master of the abstract idea, surprises me, surprises us all, by writing about the joy of hearing music for the first time after spending five years in solitary. "It was like the voice of God," he says, reading in his usual flat, quiet voice. When someone as reticent as Lee makes himself known, even in this small way, it feels like an epiphany.

The most interesting and weirdest part of the session is yet to come. It's when, apropos of nothing, Michael, Wil, and Don, who've been inside the longest, start reminiscing about an incident that happened many years ago. "The fire in the furniture factory" is how it is introduced.

"That was no fire," Michael says. "That was a murder."

"Well, it was a fire *after* the murder," says Wil. "That's when they burned his body."

I listen as they pile on details, factual and perhaps otherwise. Where they were. How they heard about it. Michael had been hiding steaks in the furniture factory, purloined from his access to the kitchen. He was worried about being found out. He was even more worried that the steaks would burn up in the fire. They are laughing, interrupting each other. Adding new memories. Michael is leaning back in his chair. Don is nodding. Wil is leaning into the group, animated. His game face is taking a time-out.

"Who was killed?" I ask.

"You mean stabbed and then burned?" Wil asks.

"I hope he was dead before he was set on fire," I say. Wil shakes his head no. Michael says the man was known as Screwdriver Jack.

"You don't want to know why he was called that," Wil says.

"Don't tell me," I say.

But Wil can't resist. "It involved children," he says.

I wince.

And then they go back to their story, entertaining each other, entertaining the other men who've never heard this tale, or this version of the tale. It is a moment of laughter and camaraderie. The incident is horrific. Yet this moment of collective storytelling seems joyful.

It's appalling. But I am not appalled. It's my new normal.

Fourteen

GLOSSARY OF PRISON SLANG

a minute: A short sentence.

backdoor parole: Dying in prison.

big bag: An eight-ounce bag of instant coffee used for trading.

birdcall: Alert that guards or other officials are coming.

blue: A convict, inmate, prisoner.

bonneroo: Nice, exceptional, as in a clean, pressed shirt.

books: Pornographic magazines.

bucket: Segregation. Also *hole, box, tomb, grave.*

Buck Rogers date: A prison sentence so long that future release is impossible to imagine. Also *Jeston set, all day, a grip, forever and a day.*

Cadillac: The best option of standard fare, as in a cup of coffee with cream and sugar, not just black.

cellie: Cellmate.

checking in: Entering protective custody.

cheeking: Hiding contraband (or medication you don't want to take) in between the cheeks of the buttocks.

chicken hawk: An older prisoner who preys on younger, vulnerable prisoners, usually with sexual intentions.

diesel therapy: Being repeatedly transported to different facilities as a form of unofficial punishment.

ding biscuit: Psychotropic medication given to mentally ill prisoners. Also *skittles.*

dog: Friend.

fall, fell: When you first go to prison, as in, "When did you fall?" "I fell in 1989."

fish: Rookie, new guy.

fishing line: A string (torn bed sheet or piece of clothing) with a weight attached to the end, thrown out of the cell to another cell with a message or an item of some kind attached.

Froot Loop: Mentally challenged inmate. Also *willy, ding.*

going to the hoop: Hiding something in your rectum—a step beyond *cheeking.* Also *going to the bank.*

gray: A guard. The official term is now CO, or corrections officer. Also *screw, man, boss, jack.*

homeboy: Someone who has served or is serving in the same correctional facility as you.

house: Cell.

house mouse: Prisoners who prefer to spend most of their free time in the cells, usually to the irritation of their cellies.

jigs: Standing watch for a friend.

paying rent: Paying someone to protect you so you can walk in the yard and feel safe.

plantation: Prison. Also *joint, slammer, Big House* (if a state penitentiary or federal facility).

pruno: Prison-made alcohol.

rapo: A sex offender.

shorts: Leftovers, once meant the last few drags on a cigarette (when smoking was permitted), now could refer to last few candies in a bag (or similar).

shuffle: The recognizable walk of a heavily medicated prison. Also *Thorazine shuffle.*

sick: Sad.

toilephone: Using plumbing pipes to communicate to distant cells (usually in segregation) by flushing the water from the pipes, then using the pipe as a voice conduit.

to the gate: Release time, as in, "four months to the gate."

two-for-ones: Loaning out goods, usually sweets, with the clear understanding that recipient will pay back double the amount.

Wall Street: A person who is connected or plugged in. Also *juiced*.
watch your six: Watch your back.

—⁓—

I could have Googled "prison slang" for this, but I don't. I ask nine men
who have, collectively, spent 235 years in prison to write down and define
the expressions they use or hear every day. The guys enjoy this exercise.
They enjoy telling stories that highlight their ingenuity, the complicated
and creative ways they and generations of others have made life work
behind bars. They are proud that they have found ways to outsmart those
who think they can control all aspects of their incarcerated lives. They
want me to know.

I listen as they read their lists out loud, as they comment, as they add
details and anecdotes. I imagine kneeling by the toilet in my cell flushing
it a hundred times, then sticking my head in the bowl and yelling down
the pipe. Because in isolation, that's the only way to communicate with
another human being. I imagine paying someone to protect me so I can
walk outside without getting hurt. I imagine life so spartan than coffee
with cream and sugar is a Cadillac version. No. I cannot imagine. Even
though I have been coming into this prison for more than a year, even
though I have listened to hours of conversation, read hundreds of stories
about prison life, even though I have heard the clang of gates closing
behind me and been subject to scans and searches and dress codes and
behavior codes, I still cannot imagine.

I know these men deserve long sentences for what they did. I also
know that they are possibly the most resilient people I've ever met. It is
difficult not to admire this resilience, to appreciate their initiative, their
resourcefulness, their ability to find humor in dark places. This is what I
see in their slang, their special language.

Fifteen

I AM SITTING AT THE KITCHEN TABLE READING THROUGH A fifty-page manuscript Sterling handed to me at the end of our last writers' group session. "I've been working on my autobiography," he told me, "and I don't know what I'm doing. Will you take a look?"

I read it through without stopping, without once looking up, and then I read it through again slowly. I am riveted by the meandering, convoluted yet gut-punch powerful narrative he has constructed out of his early life, the only part of his life he has spent outside of prison. I learn that he was born to a woman serving eighteen months in prison for forging checks. She was shackled to the hospital bed. He grew up in the house of his grandmother, the woman he called Momma, and for the next twelve years he lived a protected, churchgoing, lawn-mowing, paper-delivering, dog-walking childhood. Then Momma died, and everything changed.

I read about the wife-beating grandfather and alcoholic second wife he lived with briefly and the drug-dealing uncle he was farmed out to. He slept on the living room couch, rousted whenever the uncle and his roommate brought home women, which is to say, almost nightly. He sat outside on the porch. Or he slept in the cab of a truck. Then, when he realized no one knew or cared where he was or what he did, he took to the streets. He was thirteen. He found friends. He found trouble. "Bad deeds," he writes, "were rewarded with acts that felt good." His life began to mirror the life his uncle was living. He got shuffled to other relatives. He stole cars, took drugs, vandalized, bullied, scammed, beat up other street kids. That was the new normal.

As I read, I feel such a swell of anger toward the so-called adults in his life that I am almost sick to my stomach. I am watching a train wreck happen. I am watching a kid who had a chance turn into a thieving punk, a protogangsta, an amoral don't-give-a-fuck teen who learns life's lessons on the streets. How is it possible to fall so far and so hard? How is it possible for a young life to go so wrong? Part of me wonders whether Sterling is exaggerating—or fabricating—both the halcyon years with Momma and thrill-seeking, crime-ridden years afterward. I don't think so, but maybe it doesn't matter. It is how he remembers it, how the story unfolds in his head.

Back then, he had no idea where the casual violence, emotional deadening, and callousness of the life he was learning to live would lead. The path—and its tragic destination—seems obvious now. And Sterling, not sugarcoating anything, not denying his culpability, twenty-two years later, sees it. Or so it seems to me as I read. He sees that he accepted the notion that violence was how you proved your manhood, a lesson taught by his grandfather, by the father of his best friend, by his uncle and his uncle's friends. Not expressing emotion, seeming not to care—and ultimately not caring—was how you showed you were a man. Bragging about your exploits, the riskier and more horrific the better, got you street cred. Street cred got you respect. Respect made you a man. It made you the kind of man, or rather the kind of sixteen-year-old boy, who could murder in cold blood.

But the man that boy has somehow managed to become—at least as far as I can tell from his words, spoken and written, his manner, his attitude, his extraordinary intelligence—is a kind of walking miracle. Occasionally I'll come across a piece of writing by a prisoner or a former inmate that says something like "prison saved my life." They generally mean being incarcerated removed them from the mean streets and *literally* saved their lives. They would have been shot otherwise. Or died of an overdose. I won't say that prison has saved Sterling's life. I would say that in prison Sterling is crafting an entirely *different* life.

Inside the penitentiary, the hardened street punk who describes his adolescence as a "closed loop of run, steal, drive, party, sex, arrest," who, with a buddy, carjacked a young couple, killed them, and then bragged about it, has transformed himself into a man who sits with the dying in the prison's hospice, who mentors young African American prisoners. The kid whose high school education consisted of sitting in a room for a couple of hours in a building behind the juvenile detention center, where daily attendance was graded as "compliant" or "noncompliant," has become a diligent student of philosophy, economics, and literature—and a voracious reader. Like Lee, he has probably read more and thought more about big, challenging ideas than most graduate students. And, unlike most graduate students, he wears this knowledge lightly.

At the next writers' meeting, I hand him my four typewritten pages of comments on his biography, and he asks me if I know a Will Durant quote that goes something like "People who experience great adversity respond with either bitterness or authenticity." How much of Will Durant has Sterling read? "A lot," he says. I plowed through a volume in college and remember nothing. Later, where answers to everything are at my fingertips, I search for this Will Durant quote and can't find it. I do find something even better, I think, something that speaks to what might be possible for humans, even humans in prison, even humans who go to prison for committing murder: "The only real revolution is in the enlightenment of the mind and the improvement of character, the only real emancipation is individual."

Who Sterling is now, the middle-aged man he is in the process of becoming, does not excuse the horror of what he did. You would get no argument from Sterling about that. But who he is now stops me in my tracks. Or rather, the distance between who he is now and who I discover he was in his youth stops me in my tracks. That distance is almost unimaginably great. I wonder, if the parents of the young couple he and a friend murdered long ago could see that distance, would it make any difference to them? Would it help them to see that the senseless killing brought the killer to his senses? Would it help them move on, to find some peace? I don't know. Pain and loss are deep and permanent. It is impossible to imagine living with that. It is equally impossible to imagine living with the knowledge that you caused such pain, such extraordinary harm, to move forward from that without denying it, to summon the strength of character to remake yourself into a functioning, caring human being.

The indoctrinated-by-DOC-training skeptic might think Sterling is a manipulator. What he writes about himself is self-serving. What he does with his time in prison is a calculated act. Jimmie wrote about this after he was denied parole. He admitted that he and—he thinks— many others try to play the system, that they create an image they think the parole board wants to see, that there's no real change beneath that facade. Is Sterling presenting a facade? Is he the same inside as the kid who pulled the trigger? He just figured out how to present himself to reap whatever advantages can be reaped. I doubt it. There are really no advantages to be reaped. Or rather, there are minor advantages to be reaped by not misbehaving (level 3 privileges, A-block), but there are no institutional advantages to be reaped by coming to the writing group, by working as a hospice volunteer, by mentoring other prisoners, by helping to plan educational opportunities for others. This is not part of some paving-the-way-to-parole strategy because, as far as Sterling knows, there is no path to parole.

The same might be said of Wil and his activities in prison. Wil, the mercenary, the stone-cold killer, studied for years to become a Buddhist monk. He teaches a yoga class. He works with fellow inmates who suf- fer from PTSD. He's an on-call crisis counselor going into the cells of severely disturbed, violent, panicked men and talking them down. None of this tallies up or will ever tally up as brownie points. Wil will never get out of prison. His good works are not meant to impress a parole board, because he will never see a parole board. I can only assume that what Wil and Sterling do now, during this till-death-do-us-part grip of time they both serve, reflects the character and motivations of drastically different men than those who committed the heinous crimes that got them here.

This seems evident, yet I struggle with the idea. I think all of us non- saints struggle with the idea—the justice system itself struggles with the idea—that true, deep, meaningful, lasting change can and does happen. Some believe that the hand of God can bring about such changes. Nei- ther Sterling nor Wil claim to be saved by the Holy Spirit or transformed by giving up to a higher power. If they are transformed, it is through their own agency, through the miracle of self-efficacy.

Do I believe it? Do I believe in this kind of change? Let's say that, after a year and a half sitting in a room with these guys, of reading thousands and thousands of their words, of listening to them talk, of studying their faces, that I am open to the possibility of believing.

—᚜᚜—

Before I present today's prompt, I ask the guys to think about their strengths as writers. I'm not sure they ever get to talk about their strengths. They are surrounded by the consequences of their weaknesses.

"I have good stories to tell," says Michael, who is often the first to talk. "I mean, I have *seen* some things." Everyone laughs at that. There is a bond, well studied and documented in the sociology of prison literature, that exists among lifers, that keeps them separate from, as Michael once put it, "those guys who've only got a nickel or a dime." He was referring to those serving five- or ten-year prison sentences. Most lifers don't associate with short-timers. Lifers don't understand the world these guys come from, and they see no reason to invest their energy in building such a fleeting relationship. To a man with thirty, forty, maybe fifty years to serve, five years doesn't even register.

"We do have stories. That's so true," says Don. "But also, there's imagination. I think that's my strength. I've been here so long that so much of what I see is really in my imagination." What a startling thought. But of course it makes sense that the inner world brightens as the outer world dims. I think of Emily Dickinson. Or more to the point, Robert Stroud, the Birdman of Alcatraz (who actually had no birds in his solitary cell at Alcatraz; his bird days were spent at Leavenworth). How a big life can be lived in a very small space. Don, more than the rest of the guys, keeps long-ago images alive in his writing, and he freely embellishes them with acts of imagination. I prompted them once to finish the sentence "If I were not here right now, I would be . . . ," and he conjured up an extraordinarily vivid scene set in a restaurant he frequented more than thirty years ago: the arrangement of the tables, the view of the river from the bank of windows, the items on the menu. I have, in fact, eaten at this same restaurant, and his memory of details is amazing. He created a pretty waitress, inventing dialog between the two of them. Unlike Sterling or Jimmie, Don has never written about the dark part of his past. But this part, the eating in a restaurant with a view of the river, is very much alive.

"My strength?" says Wil. He doesn't hesitate for a second. "The ability to get to the point." He offers no elaboration because none is needed. He has gotten right to the point. He is a master of this, the unadorned observation, the Hemingway-esque sentence. A clean well-lighted place. That Wil comes to this way of self-expression from the extreme opposites—a career as a mercenary and training as a Buddhist monk—makes him one of the most enigmatic people I've ever met. And a much better writer than he thinks he is.

Sterling says his strength is the way he hears words in his head, the rhyme and rhythm, the "poetry of language." Lee points to his "conversational tone" as a strength, which is interesting to me because, of all of my writers, he writes the least conversationally. Because he so rarely writes about himself and so often writes about big ideas like ethics, moral codes, and accountability, his measured, essay-like tone is a good fit. Conversational he is not. Not even in conversation.

"I'm here," says Jimmie. He shakes his head. "That's all I can say. That's my strength." I tell him, I tell all of them, that this is enough, this is more than enough. Jimmie nods, but I can see that he doesn't quite believe me.

—◊◊◊—

I'm taking a risk with today's prompt, which is "secrets." In a way, the prompt is a test of how comfortable they are both with each other and with me. In a place where you own so little, where you have so little to call your own, it seems as if secrets would be the coin of the realm. I don't expect they will divulge any in this setting. But I hope they will allow themselves to contemplate the place secrets have in their prison lives. And I hope I will learn something.

Michael starts off. He wonders whom he might trust enough to tell a secret to. The implication is no one. Then, in the next sentence, in a quick turnaround, he states that he doesn't really want to be on the receiving end of anyone else's secrets. The burden is too heavy. The responsibility is too great. Suppose, he wonders, the secret got out somehow. He didn't tell it, but it got told. "I could be blamed," he says. "I would be considered untrustworthy." The relationship would suffer. Or worse. "It's too much to guard a secret," he says, shaking his head. I would guess that something like this has happened, but Michael doesn't want to elaborate. It's his secret to keep.

Sterling, on the other hand, seems to be the repository of many secrets. "Some I keep out of mercy for others," he says, reading from a piece of lined paper he has torn from the old-fashioned student notebook he brings to the writing group. "Other secrets I keep for trust." Although he is writing prose, he reads it as if it were poetry. He parses the lines. His voice lilts. He started writing poetry, he told me a while ago, when he was placed in solitary. He started writing to stay sane. He likes to read aloud, and he does it well. The men listen with an alertness they sometimes don't exhibit when others read. They respect him. Sterling is not the oldest (Wil has forty years on him) and he hasn't served the longest time (that would be Don with his thirty-three years). His crime is not the most gruesome—as if this would be a yardstick for anything. He doesn't hold one of the better jobs, and he isn't head of one of the clubs, like Eric who is the NA coordinator. Any one of these could be a criterion for respect among his peers. Sterling checks none of these boxes, yet perhaps second only to Wil, he is the most admired man in the room. He has charisma. There's no doubt about that. When he walks into a room—loose limbed, long haired, simultaneously relaxed and on alert—it's as if he is making a statement: Look at me. I am here in this cage, but I am not a caged man. In this room, in the writers' group, he is articulate, able to express feelings without drama, vulnerability without weakness. Wil gets respect for being tough. Sterling gets it for being tender, but in a prison-appropriate, masculine way. When he hands in his paper, I see how he has constructed his last sentence, playing with simple prose to make it something more:

> I know many things—
>   However,
>   They will remain
>   Secrets.

Kaz reads next. When he first started showing up for these sessions, he came as Michael's unofficial sidekick. In truth, I didn't take him all that seriously. I wasn't sure, other than his friendship with Michael, why he was coming. The two played off each other, joking just enough but not too much. Otherwise, he was pretty quiet. I assumed that he would drop out after a few meetings. But he keeps coming back. And he is now as intent as everyone else is on the prompts. After our last meeting, as he was walking out the door, Kaz told me that he writes poetry. I would never have guessed it. He asked if I'd like to see some of his work, and of course I said yes.

Kaz writes that keeping other people's secrets may be easier than keeping your own. "You may think you're a success fully hiding yours deep in your heart," he says, reading from his paper. Kaz writes with a pencil and prints in all caps. But secrets are "easily read" in a person's actions, he says. There are "tell-tale signs" that reveal the secrets within. I wonder what the others think. Often, but not always, after someone reads, a short discussion follows. I might comment on a particular turn of phrase or a passage of description. One of the guys might chime in with a relevant—or not so relevant—observation. No one says anything after Kaz finishes reading his short piece. It's not an uncomfortable silence, but I can't help wondering if everyone in the room is thinking to him- (or her-) self: What secrets of *mine* are easily read? What do I think I am hiding that I am not?

Jimmie has been fidgeting in his seat. I'm not sure he wants to read today. He seems to be considering the possibility, although Jimmie's brow is permanently furrowed, so I may not be reading his expression correctly. But he looks up, grabs the piece of loose-leaf paper with his freckled hand, and reads: "I'm not keeping any secrets from myself anymore." I don't know if he's written any more, but that's all he reads. Wil squints, nods.

Don is next. He writes playfully about little secrets, like the two dinner rolls he slipped up his sleeve at chow—a secret stash for later. He writes about walking past a few guys waiting for the canteen to open and not telling them the canteen is actually open so he can get in there first. A bit of information withheld. I listen to him read, enjoying his little stories, enjoying a momentarily lightening of mood in the room, glad that he finds small pleasures in these harmless actions, but also knowing that he is, in fact, a man with deep secrets. His closeted life in mid-1980s rural Oregon was a secret. Why he killed his father and brother was a secret— at least to the jury that convicted him of two counts of aggravated murder. Plus arson. (He burned down the house after the murders.) Twenty years after the fact, the lawyer who defended him wrote that Don, "a beautician by trade . . . an effeminate homosexual," was the subject of "constant ridicule" and "unremitting emotional abuse" by his retired navy father and his brother and that "at some point [he] simply couldn't take it anymore." But the lawyer did not "dare" introduce this mitigating narrative, as it is called, in Don's defense. That was because in Central Oregon at the time, writes the lawyer, "homosexuality was considered a reprehensible and inhuman act," and such an admission would have turned the members of the jury against him even before the evidence was presented. Or so reasoned the man who handled his defense. In hindsight, it's hard to see how Don's trial could have gone any worse. Don was said to have committed the double murder to get insurance money. Don's secret underlies the crime. A secret underlies the conviction.

I know these secrets because, unasked, undiscussed, unexpectedly, Don handed me an inch-thick, spiral-bound report entitled "Personal Review for Don ——" last month. The report includes long lists of Don's rehabilitation activities, his educational, licensing, and leadership certificates, letters of reference and support from his prison supervisors and various club presidents, and a 1992 letter from a state senator praising his "fine attitude about preparing yourself for the future." The packet also includes the revelatory letter from his defense lawyer, written in 2004 about the 1985 trial.

This is the same man now sitting to my left who reads about his "secret" of purloined dinner rolls. Not all writing has to scorch the soul. Some stories can be told to lighten the load. In prison it is a sanity-saving strategy to be able to do that, so I applaud Don for his lighthearted approach. And I would keep the secrets revealed in his inch-thick file. Those are his to tell or not. Yet he handed me the file. I ask him, I press him, on the subject: *Why did you give me the file?* ("I want you to understand me. I want to be understood.") *Some of the material is so personal, so sensitive; do you really mean that I am free to write about it?* ("There is nothing in that file you can't write about, Lauren.")

Still I hesitate. I wait another two weeks and ask again, quietly, when the room empties after our writing session. I specifically mention the lawyer's letter. Yes, he assures me again. "I gave that material to you. I want you to use it however you want to use it." Sometimes I am overwhelmed by the trust these men put in me: Don with his file, Sterling with his autobiography, Jimmie with his soul-bearing essays, Eric with his detailed "descent into drugs and addiction," even Wil letting me see glimpses underneath that steely facade.

Wil is the last to read. "Reasons for secrets are more important than the information withheld" is what he has written.

Sixteen

"I'M SORRY," STEVEN SAYS, SHAKING HIS HEAD, GIVING ME A sad-eyed look. "I don't have it." We are standing in front of the sign-in desk in the visitors' waiting room. I thought I was meeting him this afternoon, a few minutes before the writers' group, so that he could present me with my much-anticipated official ID badge. Just a few days ago, he had emailed that the damned thing had finally come through—more than a half year since I began the process. Now there's *another* glitch? "Just kidding," he says before my face has a chance to fall. He hands over the badge, grinning. He punches me lightly on the shoulder. I punch him back. But not so lightly. I have long ago ceased to find humor in the what-else-can-go-awry epic journey that securing the badge had become. The whole experience speaks to a system buried under layers of paperwork, hobbled by hierarchy, and so in love with rules and regulations that it has forgotten what is, or is supposed to be, at its heart: human beings. It's people like Steven and an open-faced young guard I've come to know named Cory who keep it human. But now is not the time to stew about that. Now is the time to savor a moment of victory.

I remind myself what this credit-card-sized piece of plastic (featuring a hideous picture of me) means: I can now bring in whatever materials I feel I need for the writing group—"whatever" being limited to notes, books, pens, and pencils—without sending a list and getting Steven's written preauthorization. It means that after passing through the metal scanner like everyone else, I do not need an escort to go up to the activities floor, which means I will no longer be a drain on resources. No officer—Steven or whoever might be called in his absence—will have to leave his post to come down to get me. I will henceforth be a low-impact, low-maintenance visitor. The best kind. But it also means I will be walking down two long narrow corridors, past two checkpoints (scanning my badge along the way), and across thirty-plus feet of open space, the control floor, by myself. I have never walked across control alone before. Today will be the first time. Steven rushes off to take care of business. I go through the scanner and begin the solo trek.

I am nervous.

But I am not nervous as in, "Someone's gonna grab me or shank me or drag me off." If you think like that, if I thought like that, I would never be able to set foot in the prison. Yes, there's the scary little speech I've heard every visit about the potential of harm and hostage-taking. There's my training that stressed the dangers of the place. There's every Hollywood frightfest prison movie I've ever seen. It is impossible to be ignorant of all the worst-case scenarios. But I knew early on in this work that I could not let myself frame the experience in fear. Still, as I walk across what feels like an acre of space alone for the first time, I am hyperaware of myself as a modestly but quasifashionably dressed, long-haired female, which is to say the most noticeable, noteworthy, stare-worthy sentient being of the moment. I walk with what I hope is determination. I know where I'm going. I point myself in the direction of the gate leading to the stairs up to activities. I keep my eyes focused ahead. I won't be able to see if anyone's staring at me, but I assume *everyone* is staring at me.

I catch movement out of the corner of my eye. Someone is coming toward me. I am still a good twenty feet from the gate. There's a beefy youngish guard standing there. He isn't looking my way. *Please, look my way.* The human in motion to my right is closer and now parallel, coming into my line of peripheral vision. He's a big man, well over six feet, bald. He's stepping ahead of me as if to block my way.

Wait. I know this guy.

It's Jann, one of my original writers, the funny storyteller who wrote about operating the Grill from his cell back in the old days. He hasn't been at the writers' group for many months. I heard he was having health problems. Then family issues. I sent messages through Steven, but Jann reappeared only occasionally and then not at all. And here he is. We shake hands. Other inmates are watching. Who you know is always important. But who you know in prison is more than that. It is what keeps you safe or places you in harm's way. In the middle of the control floor, with clusters of inmates making their way from one place to another but very much alert to my presence, a lifer with thirty-four years inside is shaking my hand. I'm okay.

Upstairs, Kaz, Michael, Don, James, and Lee are waiting for me. I can see them beginning to settle in. Eric catches me right before I open the door. He can't be at today's session. Once again the club he is in charge of, NA, is scheduled for the same time as the writers' group. However much Eric values the opportunity to write, Narcotics Anonymous is essential to his rehabilitation, recovery, and hopes for the future.

"I feel so guilty," Eric says after we shake hands. He is wearing that familiar worried expression. "I feel like I'm letting you down."

"You're not letting me down, Eric. Really you aren't." He looks doubtful. Actually, I don't think his look changes at all. He just looks as worried as he always looks.

"I get how important NA is. If it's where you need to be, it's where you should be," I tell him. "You are an original member of our group, a charter member. Your place is secure," I say. I'm serious but I say it jokingly to try to lighten his mood. In the meantime, I say, "Until you can come to the sessions, you can expiate your guilt by continuing to write and submit your work." As soon as I say "expiate," I regret it. The inflated vocabulary sounds pretentious. Maybe he doesn't know the meaning of the word.

Eric laughs, and for the briefest of instances the worry lines across his forehead seem to soften. "Ha," he says. "*Expiate*. That's what I'll do." Of course he knows the word. He's read more challenging books in prison than most of us read in what my guys always call "the free world." I should know enough not to underestimate these guys.

We talk for a moment about his release date. He has successfully made it through the rehabilitation hearing and the parole board review. Has he proven himself more rehabilitated, more worthy of release, than any of the other guys who've been denied, many of them repeatedly? I don't know. But I do know that he is a serious, hardworking, diligent man who is doing everything he can to set himself up for success on the outside. Success in this case means, first and above all, staying away from drugs and alcohol, and NA is the key to this.

As he is walking away to get to his meeting, leaving me to mine, he turns his head and says, almost as an afterthought, "My significant other is now my ex." What? Tara, the woman he wrote so much about, the woman whose well-being and rehabilitation he had taken on as his responsibility, the woman whose children he had hoped to be a model of sobriety for, is now his ex? This is startling news. But it does not entirely displease me. Eric had written about Tara's troubled past and troubled present, about her drug issues, her various marriages and subsequent children, her rehab efforts, her incarceration. I thought that Eric had enough on his plate already. Still, he loved her. I don't know what to say. We look at each other for a moment.

"Maybe that whole thing was just a phase," Eric says. He had hoped for a life together after release. To just let that go? But it sounds as if he has. He doesn't tell me with resignation or hurt but rather with a matter-of-fact finality. "Just a phase." Something to hold on to, to dream about, a life to imagine when release was still unimaginable. But now he can do more than dream. He can make concrete plans. Tara's the loser here, I think.

I walk into the room. I see Kaz now sitting by himself off in the corner, hacking and coughing. "Flu bug," he says between coughs. "But I want to be here. Is that okay?"

"If it's okay with the guys, it's okay with me. But I'm not going to shake your hand." He laughs. Coughs.

Michael tells me that Sterling won't be here tonight. He's in class, a university economics course, but he is talking about dropping it because it meets the same night we've been meeting. He just wants to focus on his writing, Michael says. "I told him he was nuts. I told him not to quit."

I am secretly thrilled that Sterling not only sees writing as key to his continued growth behind bars but that he also views this writers' group as a valuable tool. This man can write. He has a poet's soul and a musician's ear. He needs focus, direction—and good editing. But of course he should not drop a for-credit university class. "You're right, Michael," I say. "Please tell him I agree. Also that our meeting schedule changes, different days, different times. They won't always conflict."

The prompt for tonight is as follows: "You are warden for the day. You can change anything. What would you change?" I know I'll get some good stuff with this. My guys are experts on prison life, having spent, collectively, more than two *centuries* behind bars, most of those years here at OSP. And I know they will be both bold and thoughtful. But I am not prepared for many of their responses.

As always, or almost always, I write along with them. In this instance, I write from a place of both ignorance and privilege, a double whammy. But I have learned that the more I show my ignorance, the more one or another of the guys will step in to teach me. The more I show my ignorance, the more true conversation is possible. There is so much that needs changing in this place that I really don't know where to start. I try to imagine myself here. What would matter to me, what would be on the top of my list? I try to imagine myself as the warden (now called superintendent) of this place. What would I, what *could* I change? In my little spiral notebook, I write: Fresh fruits and vegetables. Decent lending library. If I actually lived here for twenty or thirty years, would food and books be at the top of my list? I have no idea. Five minutes fly by. They are still writing. They are writing furiously. I let them go for another five minutes, then call it.

Michael starts. Michael is beyond eager to start. "Boxing," he says. "If I was the warden, I'd bring back boxing." He's not reading from his paper, where "bring back boxing" is only one of five suggestions. (Others include separating sex offenders and gangbangers in their own cell blocks, increasing opportunities for higher education, sending all inmates into military service halfway through their sentences, and not allowing female guards to work inside an all-male prison. He doesn't think female guards are less capable. It is a matter of privacy. "Prisoners would like to keep whatever dignity they have left," he writes.)

"Boxing," he says again, nodding his head, looking around at the others for confirmation.

"You had boxing in prison?" I ask. This doesn't seem like a good idea, inmates pounding on each other, blackening eyes, bloodying lips, causing concussions.

Michael elaborates. Yes, he says, real boxing matches. "When we had boxing, you could settle things in the ring"—he pauses—"like men."

There's some discussion of memorable fights, of guys who met as enemies in the ring, duked it out, and left not as friends but with respect for each other.

"And the fight ended there," Lee says. Everyone seems to have an anecdote about this, whether directly witnessed or the stuff of legend.

But it's different these days, Michael explains. These days there's no legit outlet for the anger and hostility that are part of daily life here, for the small beefs that take on a big life inside, the slights and snubs and worse—long-standing hostilities that predate prison, racial tension, rival gangs.

"Now what happens," says Michael, "is if someone has an issue with you, you get attacked from behind. Sneaked up on."

"It's not even to hurt you," says Lee. "It's to get you in trouble."

"They send in a torpedo," Michael says. He looks over at me, knowing I won't know what he's talking about, knowing that I will ask for more so he can recount a story. It's not just that he loves telling stories. It's that he—all of the guys, really—take delight in knowing much more than I do. Me, the teacher. Me with my permanent get-out-of-jail card. I love when the power shifts this way. They are the experts here.

"A torpedo is a guy sent in, like by a gang, to punch you in the back," Michael explains.

"Not to hurt you," Lee says again.

"Yeah," says Michael. "So you're walking across the yard, and you get punched in the back, so what do you do? If you ignore it, you're weak. And that's it for you." Don is nodding. Lee is nodding. "And if you punch back, you're in trouble," Michael says. "Either way you lose. But in the ring, even when you lose, just because you were in there, because you fought, you get respect."

James reads next. He has a long list—twelve items. "Only twelve?" Michael asks, laughing.

It turns out that James's list, like Michael's, includes moving trouble-makers and gangbangers to a separate facility and increasing opportunities for education. As the superintendent of OSP, James would also raise the minimum wage for prisoners to five dollars a day (yes, that would be a raise) and mandate that 60 percent of wages go into a reentry savings account. He would increase visiting hours and make the experience less difficult for the visitors. "I am the felon," he says, reading in his quiet voice, "not my family."

Don, who has titled his response, "We're the Boss!" offers ideas everyone agrees with, including the most popular: "Get rid of layers and layers of staff." Don says inmates could do many of the jobs better than hired staff do. The guys, at various times, have talked about the cost of running the prison, the salaries of the guards/correctional officers, the (in their opinion) overly generous public employees' retirement benefits. Their opinions are stronger than their facts—they don't have access to good data—but they are not so wrong. A prisonpolicy.org study of the cost of mass incarceration lists an $80 billion price tag for operating public corrections agencies in the United States and another $38 billion to pay for the public employees who run the system. In Oregon, the corrections budget is more than $1.6 billion. I am betting the guys would be interested to know that the management to staff ratio is one to eleven. I can look up these facts. The remainder of Don's warden-for-a-day plans are sweeping in nature and, he readily admits, beyond the power of even the most powerful superintendent. If he ruled the roost, all prisoners would be granted parole after they put in their time; there would be no lengthy probation periods; and the district attorney's office would be stripped of much of its power.

Lee also focuses on the big picture, making statements about how, under his leadership, the prison would become "a model for rehabilitation and personal reform." When it's Kaz's turn, he moves the conversation back to the nitty-gritty. Increasing the number of showers per week would be his first move as superintendent. (This earns him an immediate fist bump from Michael, who gets up and walks over to the "sick corner," as he calls it, to deliver it.) Those in general population are allotted only two showers a week. I try to imagine what it would be like—what it would *smell* like—to live two to a cell, cell to cell to cell, tier on top of tier, in non-air-conditioned space where most of the windows do not open. And here I was, warden for the day, buying more books for the library.

Kaz also wants to reform and overhaul the Health Services Department in the prison. He says health services personnel can override doctor's orders from the local hospital in Salem, that they can decide whether to allow the dispensing of certain medications or the scheduling of an operation or procedure deemed necessary by a Salem hospital doctor. I don't know if he's speaking from personal experience. It sounds as if he is. Michael once told me he thought his hip replacement surgery could have been avoided had he received earlier care for persistent back troubles. It's hard to know how much of this is just second-guessing or how much might be cost containment on the part of the prison. Health Services is an impenetrable bureaucracy, and, of course, patient information is private information. But Kaz is on to something. Delivering health care in prison is a huge challenge. The population is not a healthy one, and incarceration leads to what medical researchers have termed "weathering"—accelerated aging, including earlier onset of chronic illness.

"This is my favorite prompt so far," says Kaz. Nods all around.

Apparently word spreads about the prompt, and a week later, I receive submissions from two of the guys who were not at our session, Eric and—big surprise—Jann. Eric's list calls for higher wages that allow men to help support their families, pay restitution, and establish savings for their release. He wants to see more training and educational opportunities for everyone, regardless of security level. His tone, in writing, is as serious and concerned as he is in person. It looks forward, just as he does.

Jann, who calls himself "the One Day Warden," offers so many specific reforms and so much detail about each one that it's clear he is not only a longtime resident of this institution but a serious student of its operations. He has a plan for the purchase of packages by inmates from an approved vendor to be received through and distributed by the canteen staff. He has a plan for a handheld phone system in each of the cells "with a four-foot cable attachment securing it to the wall." He wants to allow "hobbying" in the cells ("as long as no toxic materials are necessary") and would institute a tattoo school to rid the institution of the health hazard of black-market inking. He offers other ideas, from allowing non-internet-capable laptops, to reactivating an existent more lenient family visiting policy, to converting OSP to "the honor institution of the DOC" with inmates limited to those forty-five and older.

I think the men like this prompt because it is an opportunity to convert the negative to the positive, to make constructive use of all those decades of destructive experience. It gives them a chance to show their expertise in this insular world in which they have more in-the-trenches expertise than anyone else. It gives them the momentary illusion of power. The expression "the inmates are running the asylum" is an insult meaning that the people least capable of running an organization are now in charge (and is used especially when the result is chaos or calamity). But given how practical and solution-based many of these warden-for-a-day ideas are, I wonder: maybe the inmates *should* (help) run this asylum.

Seventeen

JIMMIE BRINGS ME A CUP OF WATER, UNASKED. HE'S SUCH A tough-looking guy, even now, decades past his tough-guy years. But he is also the courtliest in the group. It is a courtliness, or rather a gentleness, that is careful, purposeful, almost walking-on-eggshells-like. I think it's because he had to teach himself, in prison, as an adult, how to act—how to *be*—a "normal" person. He didn't learn this growing up in a family so violent, so bereft of a moral compass that his subsequent crimes (a newspaper story I finally, after all this time, decide to look up lists rape, assault, murder) seem like just a continuation of a story no one wants to read, a life no one wants to live. And yet he has lived it. And he brings me a cup of water, unasked.

Before we get started this afternoon, Wil announces that he must leave at "thirteen hundred" to teach his yoga class. This is quintessential Wil, the walking contradiction. I joke that when he comes back to the writing group after his class, he will bring a different kind of energy with him. I extend my arms in a low V in front of me, open my palms, and press my thumbs and third fingers together in a mudra. I take an audible breath. Wil smiles with his signature three-quarters-of-my-face-is-Botoxed smile. I am learning when I can joke with him.

The prompt today is "privacy." But before we start, I want to hear from them what I think of as the extreme "privacy"—as in isolation and solitude—of what the system calls "disciplinary segregation" or "restrictive housing" and the guys call "the hole" or "the bucket." Two of them are experts on the subject. Lee spent a total of fifty-four months in solitary confinement, punishment for a (temporarily) successful prison break. Jimmie spent a total of three years in the hole for various offenses, including fighting with an inmate, slugging a guard, and, as he wrote in a homework piece for me, "flushing a white powdery substance down the shitter."

The first thing Jimmie wants me to know about his time in the hole is that there was no *solitude* in solitary confinement. "The cells are exposed for the entire world to see into," he says, with guards and "nut doctors" constantly walking up and down the tiers. There is also "screaming, banging on metal tables, rattling bars."

Lee concurs. "What I remember most is the noise," he says. "Also the smell . . . stale mace and decaying excrement." He explains, for my benefit, that the odor of excrement came from the frequent "shit bombs" thrown by inmates at staff or into the HVAC system. "It's their only weapon." Lee summarizes the experience like this: "Total intellectual deprivation coupled with auditory and olfactory overload." In a stunning book I read, *Life without Parole*, by a man who spent twenty years in the Pennsylvania State Prison system before hanging himself, the author wrote that "at first I missed the obvious: sex, love, family and friends," and then "the next wave of what I no longer had: privacy, quiet, peace of mind."

We talk about the details of life lived in seg. Sterling and James have put in time too. Segregation is used for a variety of purposes, from punishment for violation of prison regulations to what might be thought of as protective custody (an inmate, because of youth or demeanor or outside connections, might not be considered safe in general population). Also, and most controversially, those who suffer from mental illness and are deemed a threat to themselves or others are housed in isolation units. The places might be called by different names—acronyms like SHU, IMU, RHU, MCU—but they are all separate units (prisons within prisons) with single cells where prisoners are on perpetual lockdown, meaning they spend almost every hour of every day alone in their cells. "That 'twenty-three-hour-a-day lockdown' is deceptive," Lee says. "It's more like twenty-*four* hours." He explains, from his long experience, that the one hour a day the prisoner is out of the cell is actually divided between being locked in a small shower stall and being locked in a small recreation "yard," the transit to and from conducted in handcuffs (hands behind the back), the prisoner tethered by a nylon leash and escorted by two special housing guards. Given the horrific description of the experience, it's surprising to hear Lee say that solitary confinement "barely registered." Prison had already deprived him of everything he valued, he explains. Solitary was only a little worse.

For Jimmie, it was a *lot* worse. He says he felt like he was losing his humanity, his sanity. "There was no escape," he says. "All I wanted to do was scream."

It's not difficult to find scathing reports on the psychological and physical damage of isolation on inmates. In fact, a Harvard Medical School psychiatrist named Stuart Grassian concluded that the experience of solitary confinement can cause a specific psychiatric syndrome characterized by hallucinations, panic attacks, paranoia, diminished impulse control, hypersensitivity, and difficulties with thinking, concentration, and memory. Severe depression is not uncommon. Lee says that while he was in solitary, a nineteen-year-old guy in the cell next to him committed suicide.

Wil has stories about being called into seg cells to calm down men in the throes of violent episodes, psychotic breaks, panic attacks, and PTSD-triggered moments. Recently, he says, he was called into a cell where he found a man naked except for a robe, shackled to a bed and raving. Wil is staring at the floor as he recounts this. Then he looks up, making eye contact with each of us, one by one. "What country do we live in?" he says, more indictment than question. "What century is this?"

No one says anything for a long moment. I wonder what it takes for them to tell these stories. I wonder if they have ever told these stories out loud before. They have said that they spare their family and visitors details of their life inside. That's, as Michael has said, "letting your family do your time." You don't do that. In conversations with others inside, you don't want to show your vulnerability. What you share, you carefully control. It may be that this group is one of the few places to have the kind of conversations we're having, to share these thoughts, tell these stories. Right now there is no more to say. The best thing we can do is stay quiet and write. I remind them of the prompt, privacy.

Michael asks if I am going to write too. He always asks. And, as usual, I hem and haw. I continue to worry about how my response to a prompt serves to spotlight the huge difference between the life I lead outside and the one they live inside. They lost the privilege to live the kind of life I lead. They deserved to lose that privilege. Or rather, the men they were twenty, thirty, thirty-five years ago deserved to lose those privileges. They listen (once again) to my hemming and hawing. But it's clear that they're not letting me off the hook.

We all write for the next five minutes. I look up from time to time to see their heads bowed over their papers, and I am, as I always am, overcome with pleasure. It is not just the pleasure of knowing that what they write is important to them and that they are finding expression for thoughts and ideas never before put to paper. It is the pleasure of knowing that now, at this moment, for these five minutes, they are writers, not prisoners.

Michael volunteers to start. "Privacy is just a word to me now, only a word," he reads. He stops, as if in reading those words aloud he just suddenly understood them. Don is nodding. Jimmie is nodding. "The meaning of it is something from the past, the very distant past," he says. He goes on to talk about what privacy has come to mean to him these past almost thirty years, which is mostly having his cell to himself for twenty minutes. "Taking a crap in private seems so long ago," he reads, then looks up to make sure I am okay with "crap." He continues: "I can even comfortably crap in front of a female guard.

"This is a really good prompt," he says, smiling sheepishly.

Jimmie is next. His piece begins this way: "Privacy in prison, ha, what a joke. I haven't known privacy in any of its forms for decades." He says that the only time he is ever alone is from five thirty in the morning, when his alarm clock goes off and his cellie leaves for his work shift, to six o'clock, when he leaves for work. But even those thirty minutes five days a week don't provide true solitude. He hears movement and talk, bells, clanging doors. He knows that "at any minute an unwelcome visitor can approach." Jimmie says that when he first came to prison, he had a very hard time not only with never being alone but also with always being watched, with the knowledge that cameras were everywhere. Now, he says, he lives through days, weeks, months not even realizing how everything he does is monitored. "I don't know if that's good or bad," he says, not reading but thinking aloud. Wil gives him a good, long look from across the table, one of those unreadable Wil looks that could mean anything from "I am forever vigilant and so should you be" to "I understand where you're coming from, brother." He gets up and walks out of the room. He has to meet his yoga class, but his exit is emphatic.

Lee is next, and as usual he approaches the prompt as an intellectual exercise. As much as I talk "story," he writes philosophy. As much as the other guys write about their feelings, he grapples with big ideas. It is impossible not to admire his fertile mind, the depth of his reading, his intellectual rigor. But I also wonder if the big ideas provide a screen so he doesn't have to reveal himself. Or he may be just a head-not-heart guy who experiences the world this way. Or it may be that he learned to tamp down his emotional self long ago to make life bearable inside. With this piece, Lee invokes the ideas of a thinker by the name of Emmanuel Levinas, a twentieth-century Lithuanian-born, French-educated existentialist. (And if you think I didn't have to look that one up later, you are mistaken.) Lee says, reading, that Levinas "called for an affirmation of secrecy as the actualization of personhood." The struggle to maintain a sense of personhood may be the key struggle for those who spend their lives in prison. If, as Levinas believes, one needs "secrecy" (the keeping of one's self to oneself) to be fully human, then prison does far more than take away personal freedom. It takes away personhood. Is this what Lee is saying?

Don, when it is his turn, wonders "what it would be like to be alone, by myself, not surrounded by the crush of a population always invading my space." He wonders what it would be like "to not have to stand in lines—for meals, for clean laundry, for canteen, to take a shower," what it would be like if your every movement was not watched and monitored. "What would I do in private?" he asks. "What would I feel like doing?" He stops reading, and I look at him expectantly.

"What *would* you do?" I ask.

He looks bewildered. He shakes his head. "I honestly don't know," he says. It is beyond his imagination to contemplate after thirty years inside.

Wil has unexpectedly returned early. Maybe his class was cancelled, or someone forgot call passes for the participants, or who knows what. Whatever happened, it is a reflection of that mix of rigidity and randomness that is central to this place. I don't ask Wil why he's back. He's missed listening to what most of the guys have to say about privacy, but he's heard the last bit of the conversation, and he's a little dismissive. "Prison is a culture like any culture, and lack of privacy is part of it," he says. "You learn how to operate in it." He talks about how he had to adapt quickly from a world of a one-room schoolhouse in rural Montana to a high school in the "big city" (Great Falls, population sixty thousand) and from Montana into the military. "You figure it out," he says, "and you do it." I'm not sure if I've ever heard Wil say so many sentences in a row. And he's not finished yet. "When I got here, it took me all of three days to figure it out," he says. "I walked in the yard and didn't talk to anybody. I went to chow and didn't talk to anybody. And then I beat up my cellie. That was it."

No one says anything for longer than is comfortable. When this man of few words talks, you listen without comment. You listen, and you do not question, even if his meaning is unclear. But I think I get what he means. I think he has achieved a sense of privacy by being the contradictory human being he is. On the one hand, he is so intimidating that no one, in the vernacular of the free world, invades his space. That he can continue to be intimidating at the age of almost seventy-nine, that he can continue to protect himself this way, is an extraordinary accomplishment.

On the other hand, he *feels* at home. He has found religion, Zen Buddhism; he has found a purpose, counseling vets; and he has chosen to experience incarceration with its rules and regimentation as a world familiar to him because of his long military service. And I can only assume he experiences prison the way a Buddhist would: from moment to moment, letting the conscious mind go, inhabiting only the now.

Michael reminds me that I have yet to read. I've cheated a little with this prompt. I don't write about the joy I feel in solitude, how necessary solitude is to my work, my sense of self, my equanimity. Regardless of what they might want to know about the world outside these walls, that feels too "hey, look at my amazing life I lead." So I write about how it may be possible to experience physical privacy in the outside world but that no one is private anymore in the world these men know almost nothing about and have never personally experienced, the World Wide Web world. I think this is a more insightful, perhaps a more potentially

useful take on the notion of privacy than my personal ability to seques-
ter myself. I tell them about social media and how people choose to live
parts of their private lives in public, to make themselves visible when
they could choose to be hidden, and these men who've never surfed,
Googled, posted, Facebooked, Instagrammed, or tweeted—these men
are astonished. It really *is* astonishing. I'd almost forgotten.

We've spent the last two hours talking about privacy. It makes sense
to ask them, once again, if they have any privacy concerns about me
being in their midst, me learning about their lives and writing about
those lives. The last thing I want to do after this long, slow, ongoing
buildup of trust is for them to feel blindsided by something I write. I tell
them again what my purpose is, that I want to make known this life they
are leading, that I think they may have something to say to others about
how to confront your darkest self and how not to look away.

"This is music to my ears," says Don. There is a catch in voice. "Yes,
write that. Please write that."

"Listen," says Jimmie, the tough guy, "you can write whatever you
want about me. I've told you that before." He laughs. But he means it.

"Same here," says Michael. "But I'm concerned with my victim's
family."

"You mean telling details of your crime?" I ask.

"That's not it," says Michael. "That's all public information. I just
don't think they want to know that I'm doing anything in here other than
being punished. They don't want to know I live a life."

Eric, who's just joined us for the last few minutes, his NA meeting
concluded, looks at Michael, looks down, hesitates, then decides to tell
us this story. Apparently, a while back, his adoptive parents, while waiting in the visitors' room to see him, had a chance encounter with the
family of his victim. I don't stop him for clarification here. I don't know
why the victim's family would be in the prison waiting room. Regardless,
they struck up a conversation, not knowing who each other was. When
one of his parents said they were here "to support Eric," the conversation
got dark very fast. But the door had been opened a crack, and over the
course of several months, it would open wider. The two families lived in
the same town. I am not following the details, but the wonderful conclusion of the story is that one day at the dry cleaners, one of the victim's

family members who was behind the counter came out to hug one of Eric's parents who was there to pick up dry cleaning.

"I don't know if they will forgive me," Eric says. "I don't know if they can. But . . ." He leaves the thought hanging. I look over at Michael. His eyes are red.

Eighteen

ON THE HEELS OF OUR CONVERSATION ABOUT PRIVACY AND what was okay for me to know, and especially on the heels of yet another head-not-heart response from Lee, I am startled when I start to receive thousands and thousands of words of autobiographical material from Lee. He has been telling me for close to a year that he's "working on something," but I was not prepared for what it turned out to be: a three-part, sixty-thousand-word recounting of what led to his crime, the crime itself, and the aftermath (including the successful—at least for a few days—prison break that landed him in solitary). Everything about the material is overwhelming: the sheer number of words, the relentless and precise chronicling of details, the believable-yet-unbelievable tale he tells. And the fact that he gives it to me, that he reveals himself after almost two years.

Until I read the material, all I knew is that Lee, like all my lifers, had been found guilty of murder. I had the sense that there was a significant subtext to the crime and to the case itself because Lee had received a life *without* sentence—no possibility of parole—whereas Michael, James, Jimmie, and Don had been found guilty of heinous murders, yet all their sentences included the possibility of parole. What was special about Lee's case? What was special about Lee? He had been enigmatic for so long that I had almost stopped wondering. I had certainly given up the thought that he would use writing to open up in a personal way. I had kept the promise to myself (which I hadn't been able to keep for all the men in the group) not to go hunting for information about Lee.

And then he hands me this three-part saga, each section of which provides a window into a hitherto unimaginable world inhabited by a boy whom I struggle to understand. In the story of what led up to his crime, Lee presents himself as the ethically upstanding, hardworking, innocent fourteen-year-old victim of a sick, manipulative twenty-eight-year-old man who makes him feel important and then bullies and belittles him, who enlists him in "bill collecting" and gun buying for a secret patriotic "militia," who spins wild tales of conspiracies and the Mexican mafia and assassination plots, who tries to involve Lee in robbery attempts and what appear to be money-laundering schemes, who persuades him to fleece the older man's own grandmother out of her entire life savings, and who generally, for four years, manages to insert himself in utterly creepy ways into Lee's young life. Lee states the facts. The interpretation is mine.

As I read Lee's story, I see a pitch-perfect account of domestic abuse. Although the teenaged Lee and the twenty-eight-year-old man are not lovers or partners, the relationship Lee writes about is a textbook tale of a cruel, violent, dangerous codependent liaison between unequals. As Lee writes in part 1 of this saga: "For the whole time we ran together I had tried to conform my thinking to what Robert thought. I loved Robert as a friend and wanted him to love me back." Lee figured the best way to keep and nurture Robert's friendship was not to challenge his authority. Robert, writes Lee, "used to have fun with this. He would wait for me to make a bold statement that I thought was something he would like, and then he would proclaim the opposite belief . . . heaping abuse on my stupidity." In the story Lee relates, there are a host of unsavory characters who hang around truck stops; a series of young women who seem to love Lee and then don't; a reprehensible lawyer; a corrupt district attorney's office; teachers who come out of the woodwork to proclaim what a terrible kid he was. If someone made a movie of this or wrote a novel based on this, no one would believe it.

I am having a hard time believing it.

This may very well be true. It's not that I think Lee is lying. It's that, in part, the man he killed is presented as so unrelentingly awful, so full of improbable tales, so scheming and deeply psychologically sick that it is difficult to understand how everyone around him didn't see this, how he got away with all Lee says he got away with. I can see how Lee, with limited life experience, an early high school dropout living a motherless, hardscrabble life, how fourteen-, fifteen-, sixteen-year-old Lee might be caught in this older man's web. But what about Lee's father? Or any of the investigators who later came to be involved in the case? It is not just that in this recounting, Lee's own lawyer seems bent on his client's destruction. It is not even the challenge of wrapping my head around the notion that Lee could come to believe that he had no choice other than to kill Robert. ("Silence in the face of evil is itself evil." An anti-Nazi German pastor said that. This is, essentially, Lee's internal monologue as he persuades himself that he must rid the world of the evil that is Robert.)

This is difficult to make sense of, but what also challenges me is Lee's precise, meticulous recounting of the story. With pinpoint detail, exhaustive detail, he narrates events that took place in the mid-1990s. He writes, for example, about the time, the *sixth* time, Robert took him to pick up rifles from his boss, the man Robert told him was "commandant" of this secret, private militia. It is nine at night when they pull into the apartment complex. Lee notes the make and model of a car that drives by and the race of the man in the driver's seat. He lists and describes everyone who is in the apartment, what they are wearing ("immaculate oversized Dickies trousers"), the furniture in the living room. And this is not even, compared to what follows, a particularly significant event. There are hour-by-hour recountings of trips into the woods with Robert (presumably Lee is helping him escape or hide out from alleged assassins), verbatim conversations, blow-by-blow (literally) accounts of "friendly" tussles and roughhousing that turn violent, or real fights that begin with shouting and accusations. Who threw the first punch, who kicked whom and where, who shoved whom and into what, the date and time of every altercation, the location of wounds and bruises. Some people have excellent memories. Some people—they are called hyperthymesiacs—have an almost bizarrely detailed autobiographical memory. It's a brain wiring thing, according to neurobiologists who study the phenomenon. Is Lee is a hyperthymesiac?

It is probably more likely that he has access to his own past testimony and that he has had a prodigious amount of time to think about, construct, and reconstruct the narrative of this time in his life. Memory, as Freud has said, is a transforming, reorganizing process, essentially a creative process. Lee is writing to make sense of the story, to square the story with his own beliefs about himself. It is the way all humans revise and refashion memory.

However he came to the story he tells in the sixty-thousand-word, three-part saga, the official record tells a very different story. I decide to check Lee's record only now after I have read his story. There's no point in remaining ignorant of the publicly available information on the case. When I take the plunge, I discover it is not hard to find quite a bit of information about Lee. In fact, his was a notorious case. Lee received the longest prison sentence in the history of the state (five lifetimes without parole). The record states that Lee beat up (eleven broken ribs) and tortured (carburetor fluid in the face) Robert in an effort to extort money. Robert pressed charges. Then, three days before he was set to testify against Lee, Robert disappeared. Lee and an accomplice had taken Robert to a remote location where Lee sledgehammered him, tried to slit his throat, and then tossed him into a shallow grave. It is always a shallow grave. Robert may or may not have still been alive. Here Lee's version of the events exactly matches the official account. He does not shy away from the grizzly details. He takes full responsibility for the planning and execution of the crime. It is everything before the crime that is different in his telling of this tale.

The court record paints Lee as a diabolical psychopath. Lee understands himself as the *victim* of a diabolical psychopath. That both stories end the same way—the brutal murder of Robert, the lifetime incarceration of Lee—makes the tale less, not more understandable. I turn this over in my head for weeks. The extraordinary incongruity is harder for me to process than the other incongruities I have faced during the time I've spent getting to know these men: the juxtaposition between the deeply insightful and caring man I see in Sterling and the violent, amoral braggart he was when he committed his crime; the generous, self-effacing man I see in Michael and the violent, abusive husband he was; the sweet-tempered, diligent man I see in Don and the man who murdered his father and brother and torched their house. I think it's because I can frame these other incongruities as before and after, the after being the result of the slow, painful, decades-long process these men went through to face themselves and try to understand what they did.

With Lee, there doesn't seem to be a process. Or it may be that the process is just now beginning. He believed killing Robert was the only decent and moral thing he could do, his only choice, and he still sees it that way. He made what he thought of as a moral choice, and he sticks by it. Throughout the three-part tale, written now more than twenty years later, he identifies as a cruelly manipulated victim who felt he had to take justice into his own hands. But at the conclusion of part 3, it seems that Lee's forty-year-old self is just beginning to entertain some doubts. "Looking back I have to question everything I thought I knew," he writes. What he appears to be questioning is Robert's presentation of himself, the stories he told about the militia and the Mexican mafia, about the plots against him, those wild tales that fascinated and ensnared the teenaged Lee. Maybe they weren't true. Maybe Robert wasn't who Lee thought he was. "These misplaced beliefs compromised my decision-making process," he writes. "Not only am I responsible for the things I did. I am responsible for being in error about these things." Maybe the murder is one of "these things." Maybe he is referring to his interaction with his lawyers, the decisions he made about not taking a plea bargain when he could have, the confusion around the bail his father posted and under what circumstances it could be returned. (This is a major—and confounding—part of the story.) That Lee remains unrelenting in his acknowledgement of guilt makes him "credible." That his version of events prior to the murder is in direct opposition to the narrative told by the prosecution and believed by the jury makes him not credible. Yet the quiet man in my writing group seems sane and reliable, smart, studious, and even tempered.

For as long as I've been running this writers' group, I have wanted to be let into the world these men inhabit. And now Lee—following Michael, Don, Sterling, Eric, Jimmie—has let me in. And I want to look away. But I can't.

Nineteen

MONTHS AGO, WHEN MICHAEL INVITED ME TO BE PRESENT AT his rehabilitation hearing—known more chillingly as a "murder review" hearing—he warned me. "It's going to be brutal." Then he added, "You don't have to come." Then he said, "You might not want to come."

His warnings didn't scare me. I knew Michael. I knew what he had done, the brutality of what he had done, and I thought I understood better than most the workings of the system that was punishing him for what he'd done. I told myself that I could handle it, whatever "it" turned out to be. Of course I wanted to come. I was honored—if that's the right word—that Michael would ask me. I thought it said something about his trust in me. And it certainly said something about Michael's willingness to expose himself, to make his darkest self knowable to me, to allow me to witness him at this most singularly vulnerable moment.

Although I was not as innocent as I once had been about the crimes the men had committed, I had not asked them for, nor purposely sought out, the exact details of the crimes. I knew the specifics of Lee's crime only because he had written about it with unnerving precision and had shared that writing with me. Sterling had also written a (far less detailed) description of the night he and a friend carjacked a young couple and shot them. James had written a lot about his shame and his regrets but almost nothing about what had happened the night he murdered a young woman who was his friend. One of the first things Eric had written about was his addiction and the car accident he caused, but he provided few details. Jimmie had told me, when we first met, that if I knew what he had done, I wouldn't let him in group. I honored his wishes by not trying to discover the who/what/when/where/how of his crimes. Neither Don nor Wil had ever referenced their crimes in any writing, although the thick file Don had given me, which included his former lawyer's letter, provided the facts.

I felt that this was their backstory to share or not. What they all wrote about were the consequences of their acts. They lived the consequences. My focus was on their lives now, how they lived them, how they became who they were today. This hearing was about whether Michael was capable of rehabilitation, so I believed its focus would be the last three decades of his life. I thought whatever happened at the hearing would provide insight into how—or if—he had come to terms with what he did, how he thought about that man who had killed his wife, that man who, presumably, he no longer was. Michael told me there would be a lot of testimony and questioning about the night of the murder. He didn't have to make it so easy for me to find out the details. It was, I thought, an act of bravery. Would I ever, could I ever, invite someone to learn about my darkest self?

Attending the hearing of the parole board was also a way for me to observe the system that ruled these guys, that determined whether they would ever walk out the front door. I had already read about the hearings structure in both the impenetrable Department of Corrections documents and the rehab worksheets written for inmates with dumbed-down statements like "rehabilitation takes a lot of time and work on your part." I had heard about the hearings secondhand through the tangled experiences of the guys. Jimmie had been denied. Wil had apparently been denied. He once told me, in passing, that the board told him never to come back. *We're never letting you out,* they said. Don had been found rehabilitatable on one count but not the other, which I won't try to explain because it is inexplicable. Eric, on the other hand, had been successful and was slated for parole. Now I would have the chance to observe firsthand. And I would see Michael in a setting other than the activities floor room we sat in twice a month.

At this point, Michael had already served twenty-eight years of what had originally been a life without parole sentence that, after a complicated appeal in 1993, had been changed to life with the *possibility* of parole after thirty years. This hearing was a step in the "possibility" direction.

A three-person subgroup of the parole board would hear evidence to determine whether they believed Michael was "capable of rehabilitation within a reasonable period of time." (If deemed capable, then he could be scheduled for a parole hearing.) He had already gone through one rehab hearing at the end of 2012, the result of which was that the board unanimously found it was "not reasonable to expect that the inmate would be granted a change in terms of confinement before four years." In prison lingo, the board had given him a four-year flop, which meant they didn't want to see him again, and he couldn't try again, for four years. It was now four and a half years later. Would he be deemed "rehabilitatable" at this hearing?

What that meant exactly was—is—unclear. When we talked about rehabilitation in the writers' group, some of the guys had definite ideas. For James it was all about working hard, working overtime, and showing a healthy bank account. For Don it was about amassing educational credits, getting degrees. For Jimmie it was about joining every therapeutic, prosocial group there was, about embracing religion. A few months ago, I had used "rehabilitation" as a prompt, and even those who were conducting their prison lives as if there were some rehab checklist struggled figuring out what it meant.

"Are you dangerous? Am I dangerous? I wonder what determines that," wrote Don.

James wondered, "Will I ever get out of prison? It's a tricky question," one that will be decided by "people tasked with getting to know me in my entirety in the span of 2–3 hours."

Sterling, ever articulate, was "weary of naysayers who believe behavior is fixed." For him rehabilitation was about transformation and growth. But how to measure that?

Jimmie saw the other side of that and wrote with the bitterness and cynicism of experience. Those in authority use the promise of rehabilitation to "control and manipulate," he wrote in his perfect cursive script. Those seeking parole, he wrote, take courses or go through therapy not for "the benefits of transformation" but to present "certificates of achievement."

For Michael, who back when he wrote on the prompt was already planning for the hearing, rehabilitation was a "state of mind." He acknowledged its "undefined standards."

Everyone nodded—Sterling slapped his palm against the table in agreement—when Kaz read his piece aloud: "To most of us here in prison rehabilitation is a seldom defined set of requirements with unknown parameters."

—⁜—

That might even be an understatement. Within the world of US corrections—the vast prison system itself, the philosophies and theories of incarceration, the research, the politics—there has long been deep ambivalence about both the concept and the realities of rehabilitation. Retributive justice, exacting a price from those who offend (the "eye for an eye" approach) was replaced in this country long ago with the philosophies of deterrence (the example of incarceration will head off future criminal behavior) and incapacitation (the separation of offenders from society will protect society). The notion that offenders could transform into law-abiding citizens—the essence of rehabilitation—underlay that nineteenth-century prison experiment in Philadelphia, that place of solitude and isolation designed to inspire regret, self-reformation, personal transformation. The solitary confinement of all prisoners, the lack of contact and communication with all others, were Draconian measures, cruel and (as we now know) psychologically damaging measures, but the intent was rehabilitation. The belief was that rehabilitation was possible.

Later, much later, therapeutic and educational programs were introduced in prisons, again with the belief that rehabilitation was possible. But it was a rocky road. Rehabilitation efforts cost money. Conservatives argued that these programs "pampered" prisoners. Liberals argued that they equaled mind control. Others were upset that publicly funded counseling, therapy, and education programs in prisons meant that inmates had more opportunities for self-improvement than law-abiding folks. Then the debate came to an abrupt halt in 1974 with the publication of—and extraordinary publicity around—a study by sociologist Robert Martinson. Entitled "What Works?," the study examined the effectiveness of prison rehabilitation programs around the country. The answer to "what works," according to Martinson, was nothing. Rehabilitation efforts did not work. Rehabilitation programs had minimal or no effect on whether prisoners, once released, would commit new crimes.

Martinson, a previously obscure professor, became a temporary media darling. He was featured in *People* magazine and interviewed on *60 Minutes*. His study, widely quoted, touted as proof positive of the forever-damned mind-set, ushered in what various historians of incarceration have dubbed the "nothing works period." The very next year, 1975, the conservative social scientist James Q. Wilson's book *Thinking about Crime* posited that criminals—he called them "wicked people"— were fundamentally different than the rest of us, that criminality was so deeply rooted in their makeup that nothing could be done except to "set them apart from innocent people."

The mood was clearly shifting, more like stampeding, away from rehabilitation. The result was the removal of many educational and rehabilitation services—and even exercise equipment—from prisons. Although Martinson published an article five years later qualifying his 1974 findings, recanting his generalizations and confessing to serious methodological flaws in the original work, this subsequent research got scant attention. The belief that there was no way to make bad people better fit too well into the "get tough on crime" political agenda of the 1980s and 1990s.

Yet, America was, and is, the land of second chances. Of second acts. A country of people who left one life behind to craft a new, better one. How does this square with "nothing works"? With the belief that transformation is not possible? The contradictions seem irresolvable. And so the debate over rehabilitation continues to play out in the political arena as it plays out every day behind the concrete walls that separate us from those who have harmed us. It is hardly surprising that prisoners like the guys in my writing group don't have a clear indication of what being rehabilitated means or that the corrections and parole systems don't have transparent guidelines. How do you define something you may not believe is possible? How do you measure it? But definition and measurement were what the hearing, Michael's hearing, was supposed to be all about.

—◊◊◊—

I have to make advance arrangements to attend the hearing, which, the DOC information states, is open to anyone. That they may be, but in fact, almost the only people who attend these hearings are either advocates for

the prisoner (his lawyer, family loyalists, character witnesses) or advocates for the victim's side (the prosecutor, victim's family and friends). I
will be attending as an observer only. Still, I want to make sure that my
attendance doesn't somehow jeopardize my volunteer status. In training, we heard about volunteers who stepped over the line by becoming
overly involved in the lives of prisoners and, as a consequence, had their
ID cards rescinded. Given how long it took me to secure the card and
how it eases my comings and goings, I don't want to make a mistake here.
I check all the information given to me in training, and I read over my
notes. I check with Steven, who also checks the rules and checks with
his supervisor. As long as I am attending as an observer and not giving
testimony, there's no problem.

The hearing begins at eight thirty. At quarter past eight, I am standing at the counter in the waiting room presenting my ID badge to the
officer on duty and wondering if all these people—I count close to
twenty—are here for Michael's hearing. It's not visiting hours, and there
are no activities scheduled for this early time slot, so they must be. It's
easy to pick out who the two attorneys might be. They're the guys in suits
hefting thick file folders. I figure the particularly well-put-together man
is from the Washington County DA's office, the people who prosecuted
the original case, and is here to argue against the idea that Michael could
be rehabilitatable and have a chance to get paroled. The other guy, short,
squat, a little rumpled, looks a lot like Joe Pesci in his *Goodfellas* days.
(Later he tells me people have stopped him on the street to ask for his
autograph.) This has got to be Michael's attorney. We eye each other. He
is very curious about me. And I am very curious about him. It turns out
that he is new to the case. He wasn't the attorney Michael had for the 2012
hearing or, decades earlier, for his trial. He gets a modest stipend from
the parole board to represent Michael. The stipend pays for ten billable
hours, which, he tells me, includes the two hours back and forth from
his Portland office. I tell him about the writers' group. Will I testify for
Michael? he asks. There is hope tinged with a bit of desperation in his
voice. I can't do that, I tell him.

In the midst of our conversation, I study (without, I hope, seeming
to) the more than a dozen people gathered around the other attorney.
They must be relatives of Michael's wife, his murder victim. It's been

almost three decades since the night of that crime. They haven't forgotten. Who could? I suspect that they are here for one reason: to argue against any possibility for Michael's release. Most of them are older and look like hard-worn, working-class folks. There's one younger woman, pale, fleshy, who looks a lot like Michael.

We're processed through the TSA-style metal screener, led down the long hall and through two metal gates to a locked door, then up a narrow stairway into just the kind of room—bleak, institutional—you'd expect to find inside a prison. In front of the room, behind a long table, sits the three-person panel: two men and a woman. They're staring at their laptops. In front of the long table are two chairs. Michael's attorney takes one and begins opening folders and studying documents. The rest of the room is arranged in two sections of aged folding chairs set up in rows at ninety-degree angles to each other. One section, now filled, is designated for the victim's side. The other, nearly empty, is for Michael's side. This is where I sit because there is no place set aside for observers. The only other inhabitants of this section are an older woman who tells me she is from the Oregon chapter of CURE (Citizens United for Rehabilitation of Errants) and a guy named Andy who will be offering testimony—the only one on the docket—in support of Michael.

Near the back of the room, in the corner, is a cage the size of a phone booth. At the back of the cage, set into the wall, is a door that apparently leads to an adjoining room. The door opens. Michael fills the small doorway, steps into the cage, and stands there until an officer unlocks the front section. He is ashen. His eyes are glassy. He's a big, lumbering man who looks bigger in the oversized prison T-shirt that balloons around his bulky middle and a pair of ill-fitting, saggy prison jeans. His head is freshly shaved and is glistening with sweat. His wrists are shackled together. He walks slowly, with a slight limp, the result of the hip replacement surgery he had last year. His broad shoulders slump forward. He looks at me and nods almost imperceptibly, then, with some difficulty, settles himself on the chair next to his attorney. He is a big man in a small chair. It makes him look intimidating. His back is facing me. I am perhaps ten feet away. I can see his shoulders move up and down. He is taking deep breaths. When he is sworn in, he has to bring his left hand up with his right because they are shackled together.

Michael's attorney delivers a brief opening statement, recounting the history of the case and referencing the severity of the crime. "He murdered [his wife] in a horrible way," he says. "We are not arguing the facts." But the "preponderance of evidence" shows that Michael is capable of rehabilitation. The lawyer's delivery is interesting, a combination of straight-ahead, just-the-facts-ma'am professional and conversational, as if he is having a personal exchange with the panel. He is formal and informal. You can tell he's done this before. Many times. In fact, as I discover during the one break in the proceedings, he is scheduled for an afternoon hearing today as well.

As I listen I am suddenly, acutely—unnervingly—aware that I am observing the lawyer, studying Michael, tracking the people in the victims' section as if I were watching a play or a TV drama. But I'm not. This is Michael's life. This is Michael's future. Despite the sheen of sweat on Michael's bald head, the room is chilly. My hands are icy.

The lawyer concludes by saying that when the 2012 panel gave Michael a four-year flop, they deemed him "stoic and unemotional." "But he feels deeply. He feels pain." The lawyer looks over at Michael, who is seated just an arm's-distance away to his left. He doesn't know Michael. He has spent a total of one hour with Michael: a half-hour in-person visit and a half-hour phone call is what Michael tells me later. But the lawyer is right about this. I know he's right: Michael is in pain. He can't escape it. He is staring at his knees. I look over at the victim's side. Their jaws are set.

Andy, Michael's first and only witness, is a former volunteer who used to help organize basketball tournaments that Michael (younger, with a good hip) used to play in. Andy comes across as a good-hearted fellow who likes Michael but has very little insight into his character. The conversations they had years ago were not deep or soul-searching. The lawyer tries hard, quizzing Andy about what he sees in Michael that makes him believe he is rehabilitatable. The testimony seems weak to me, not because Andy doubts Michael—he clearly is a supporter—but because he can't come up with specifics. He relies on prison-speak, referencing Michael's "prosocial behavior" and "clear conduct." I assume he's here not because he was deemed a great witness but because there was no one else. For the 2012 hearing, Michael's biological father (now dead) testified by phone, and a psychologist Michael hired testified, telling the panel, apparently unconvincingly, that Michael was "already there" in terms of rehabilitation.

Now the attorney faces Michael, and this phase of the questioning begins.

"Are you nervous?" he asks.

"Absolutely," Michael says, almost in a whisper. He is looking down at the floor.

"Make eye contact," the attorney says, softly, to Michael, but loud enough for me to hear. The panel probably hears this too.

He takes Michael through a recounting of his childhood—single mom, mostly raised by grandparents, lower middle class. Michael says, "I had a dream childhood," but then contradicts himself without seeming to realize it by admitting to an early problem with alcohol and expulsion from high school just before graduation for being caught with a gallon of vodka in the school parking lot.

The attorney then shifts the questioning to Michael's relationship with Brenda, his wife, the murder victim: where and how they met, the details of their marriage, the birth of their two daughters, his role as husband and father. Michael repeatedly calls Brenda "a great woman, a great mother." I study the young woman in the front row of the victims' section, the one with Michael's coloring, Michael's soft, round chin. She winces when he says this. Her hand rests on the thigh of an older woman sitting next to her who several times puts her arm around the young woman's shoulder.

Michael says he worked hard, worked overtime to provide for his family, that he saw himself as the boss of the family. "So you were to be obeyed?" asks the lawyer.

"Yeah," says Michael. "It was my way or the highway." Yet in response to the lawyer's next question, he says he wasn't "controlling." This is, I am getting an inkling, a code word. It's the word that stands in for domestic abuse or at least opens the door to a recognition of it. The record shows Michael hit his wife, giving her a black eye once and a split lip another time. If he denies being "controlling," if he doesn't see that this was his behavior, even now almost three decades later, how can the parole board view him as a changed man? As rehabilitated—or rehabilitatable?

It's only twenty minutes into the proceedings. Things don't seem to be going well.

What emerges as Michael answers his lawyer's questions is the difference between how Michael understands and talks about his life versus how educated professionals well versed in behavior and criminality—like the lawyers, like the members of the parole panel—understand the circumstances. The record portrays Michael as uncaring, uninvolved, absent from family life most of the time. But he, in response to the lawyer's question, calls himself a loyal family man. That's because Michael's definition of family man means taking on extra shifts at work to bring home a bigger paycheck. The world of his youth and young adulthood, his semirural, hunting-gun-in-the-rack-of-the-pickup-truck preincarceration world, formed who he was. Maybe who he still is. Prison, his home for most of the past three decades, has not provided a culturally enriching learning environment that could have broadened these horizons.

The lawyer is now focusing on the crime itself, taking Michael through every detail. Michael says he was very drunk when he attacked and killed his wife, that he was drinking with buddies all day and then downed a six-pack on his way over to where his wife and daughters were staying. This, I guess, makes the attack seem somewhat less horrific. People do horrible, horrible things when they are drunk. Alcohol, as those who study its effects have said, "releases aggressive impulses from their cortical inhibition." Later, reading a book called *After Life Imprisonment*, I am struck by the author's comments after observing a number of parole hearings. Even though pointing to external causes for behavior—drinking, drug use, abusive parents, for example—is "normal and frequently healthy," she writes, parole boards are looking for a different narrative. They want the prisoner to "point the finger at themselves." Regardless of extenuating or even mitigating circumstances, they want to hear the prisoner take full responsibility. That's not what they are hearing from Michael this morning.

And there is an inconsistency in this under-the-influence version of the night of the murder. Blood samples from the crime scene, introduced as evidence in his trial, show no trace of alcohol in his blood. The lawyer notes this. He has to. It's in the record, and the panel knows the record. Michael says he can't explain it. But there may be an explanation.

Michael mumbles this under his breath, but the lawyer doesn't pick up on it. It could be that the samples were taken after Michael was given four pints of whole blood at the scene. (After he stabbed his wife, he slashed at himself and was bleeding profusely.) I want to believe this explanation because I don't want to believe—I don't believe—Michael is lying about his drinking. The "I was drunk" statement doesn't change (or in any way excuse) the crime. But as the record stands now, Michael's testimony about being drunk appears to be a lie. And if he is lying about this, the panel may be thinking, what else might be lying about? And if he's a liar, how does that square with being rehabilitatable?

Michael continues answering the lawyer's questions about the murder. Did he kick down the door of the trailer? Yes. Did he threaten her? Yes. In front of his young daughters? Yes. Did he drag her out the door? Michael is sobbing now. He reaches with his right hand for a wad of tissues stuck in the back pocket of his sagging jeans. Because his wrists are shackled, he has to torque his left shoulder, swivel his torso, and wrap his left arm across the expanse of his belly to reach into his pocket. His fingers grope for the tissue, but he can't quite reach it. He twists his torso as far to the right as he can, reaches again. The room is silent. Everyone is watching him. After another try, he manages to extricate the tissue from his pocket and wipe his eyes.

Finally the questioning moves on to what Michael has done to transform himself from a killer to a man who can safely be set free. With each question the lawyer asks, I silently answer for Michael, constructing a response based on both how I understand him and what I think the panel wants to hear. Michael, however, doesn't answer this way, and his responses are not doing him any good. Yes, he joined AA and NA, but he no longer attends meeting because he "had issues with some of the people involved." So the message to the panel is that he doesn't know how to resolve these issues and that, although he says he's an alcoholic, he is not staying with "the program." (The truth to why he dropped the program is far more complicated and less damaging to his case, but Michael doesn't tell it. He would be ratting out fellow inmates. This is what he tells me later, and I have many reasons to believe him.) In answer to how he has changed from being angry and controlling, Michael responds with specific anger management strategies, not life-changing insights. He knows how to step back and take a breath. He knows to think before he acts. He has taken anger management classes. The panel is looking for a different kind of self-awareness.

For the next hour, the three members of the board, in succession, pepper him with questions. The woman is first. Her name is Patty Cress, and, as I discover later when I look her up, she has worked as a parole and probation officer specializing in domestic violence and sexual offenders. That background, and the in-the-trenches understanding that comes with it, informs her every question, most of which are focused on getting Michael to admit that he is—or was—an abusive husband before the murder, that the murder was not some ghastly isolated act but rather part of a pattern of abuse that defined the marriage. Michael either doesn't understand what she's getting at or he doesn't understand that he was, in fact, an abusive husband. If the former, then my sympathies are entirely with him. He just doesn't have the vocabulary. He is playing out of his league. If the latter, then he truly has yet to understand himself and come to terms with who he was.

"You're an extreme case," Cress says. The words are harsh, but she delivers them so matter-of-factly that it takes a moment for me to register how harsh they are. What does Michael hear? I can't see his face. "We need to know how you think you've changed," she says. At last, a direct question, an open door.

I want Michael to step through. I know him, I think I know him, through his writings, through his interactions in the group and with me. He listens. He is solicitous and kind to the other men. He has a sense of humor. He has humility. I want him to show this to Patty Cress. Instead, he hesitates. "Well," he says, "there's not much programming in here to help." He is thinking only of the domestic violence aspect. He mentions that he tried to get someone to come in and do a workshop on domestic abuse. He was in the prison infirmary recovering from his hip replacement when she came. He tried. That's good, I think. But this was the entirety of his effort to deal specifically with domestic violence during his twenty-eight years behind bars? Patty Cress is busy typing on her laptop.

The next questioner is Michael Wu, a former deputy DA and drug court prosecutor. He is especially kind. "I know this is stressful," he says.

He looks squarely at Michael. His questions, too, are about domestic
abuse and violence. He is going over the same ground, giving Michael
a chance to be clearer, more insightful, more convincing. But Michael
continues to portray himself as a hardworking, hard-drinking guy who
didn't communicate well and got very angry. All true. But he is not owning the "domestic abuse" label. They want him to own the label. Finally,
after two and a half hours, most of which has been focused on the crime,
Michael says the magic words. "I am a batterer." But then he quickly
moves to the anger management strategies and communication tactics
he has learned.

"Is that what's about?" Wu asks. "Coping strategies?" Clearly Wu
doesn't think so.

The third panelist, Sid Thompson, is a career corrections guy, former
regional director of a private corrections company, a corrections consult-
ant with his own firm, a former superintendent of MacLaren Youth Correctional Facility, famous (or infamous) for having housed Kip Kinkel
and, before that, Gary Gilmore. Should those names be unfamiliar to
you, I suggest you stay ignorant. If this were a court of law, what Thompson does next might be interpreted as badgering the witness.

"I don't understand why you found it necessary to kill Brenda," he
says. This is his opening remark. "You say she was a 'beautiful, kind,
caring person.' I'm sorry, but did you think this when you stabbed her?
How could you love your family and have this be a core value and then
grab your wife in front of your two young daughters?"

—m—

For most of the next two hours, including a short break, five witnesses
from the victim's side testify. Each one, when called, takes a seat in a folding chair to the side of the panelists' table. This puts them perhaps eight
feet from Michael. They do not look at him. He does not look at them.

First is Brenda's brother, well dressed, articulate, reading from a very
long, very carefully constructed document that cites, in great detail, the
trial record, the testimony from the 2012 hearing, the findings of that
hearing. Michael's lawyer had told me before the hearing began that each
witness is limited to five minutes but that, especially with the victim's
side, the time limit is never enforced. Brenda's brother has been reading

for twenty minutes. He is gently reminded that the document he is reading from has been submitted and is part of the record. He keeps reading,
now recounting the details of the night of the murder. His voice quavers.
He stops. Behind him, in the first row of the victim's section, the young
woman who looks like Michael is crying. The older woman sitting next
to her hands her a tissue.

Then that woman, the older woman, takes her place at the table to
give testimony. It turns out that she is Brenda's sister. She raised both of
Brenda and Michael's children, who were two and three at the time of the
murder. She looks tired, spent, as if her whole life has been a struggle. Her
voice is steady, flat, under control. "Brenda doesn't get a second chance,"
she tells the panel. "Why should he?" She says the family will not feel safe
if Michael is released. She thinks he will seek revenge. Michael is motionless in his chair, his head bowed, his shoulders slumped. His shackled
wrists hang below his knees.

In one of our writers' sessions a while back, the talk turned to recidivism and how likely it was that someone convicted of murder would
commit a crime—murder or otherwise—after being paroled. I think
it was Sterling who said he thought that the recidivism rate for murderers was the lowest of all. I checked. A report from the Bureau of Justice
Statistics a few years ago found that more than three-quarters of drug
offenders were back in jail five years later, but just 2 percent of convicted
murderers went out and murdered again. An award-winning journal-
ist named Nancy Mullane studied recidivism rates, specifically among
murderers, for her book, *Life after Murder*. Investigating the records of
almost a thousand convicted murderers released from prisons in California during a twenty-year period, she found that 1 percent were arrested
for new crimes. None were re-arrested for murder. There is data—and
I'm betting the members of the parole board are familiar with it—and
then there is the power, the gut-punch power, of hearing a murdered
woman's sister say that she fears for her life.

And then there is Antonia. That's the name of the young woman in
the front row, the woman who has Michael's pale coloring, his fleshy face.
She walks up to the chair set aside for witnesses and turns it forty-five
degrees to the right before she sits. Now, instead of the side of her body
facing Michael, her back is to him. It is a small, purposeful act. I read it

as part defiance, part self-preservation. She is Michael's oldest daughter. She was three when her father grabbed her mother, pulled her outside, stabbed her, ran after her, stabbed her again.

Just Antonia's presence is enough. She doesn't really have to say anything. But she does. She recounts how her father has tried to reestablish contact with her and her sister and how unwanted and frightening those efforts have been. I know about these efforts. Michael has told me (and the 2012 hearing documents show) that he saved money from his hundred-dollar-a-month prison job to buy a computer and arranged to have it sent as a gift to his daughters. He also sent Antonia a tooled leather bag he designed in hobby shop. Michael saw this as reaching out, as trying to open the door, maybe a crack, to future communication. He was not supposed to make contact with his daughters, he knew that, but he still thought of himself as a father; he still wanted to be a father. And he had read about and thought about "restorative justice," which is based on conciliation between offenders and victims. But these unwanted gifts felt like acts of aggression to the daughters. It scared them. They didn't want their father to know anything about them. They didn't want him to know where they lived. "He keeps reaching out," Antonia tells the panel. "He has used other people to get to me. If he gets out . . ." She pauses to take a breath. "I don't want to live in fear for the rest of my life."

Two more of Brenda's family members testify before the lawyer representing that side, the senior deputy DA who has represented the family before, makes his remarks. After the family's testimony, he doesn't have to say much. But he does add this one horrific fact from the night of the crime. Michael had broken into his mother-in-law's trailer, where his wife and daughters were staying, and was standing in the living room yelling and threatening. The youngest daughter, the two-year-old, was on the couch. In an effort to defuse the situation, the mother-in-law picked up the little girl and held her up in front of Michael. "Michael, please, this is your daughter. Don't do this." She pleaded with him, the lawyer says. He is recounting this deadpan. It is not necessary to add drama. He lets that sink in, the image of the little girl and the big, angry man with the knife hanging from his belt. "This level of animal behavior is not fit for society," he says. I stare at Michael's back, his bald head.

He can make a final statement now, but he doesn't know what to say that he hasn't already said. He is sorry. He is crying. "Brenda, I loved you," he says. Antonia flinches. "I am so sorry for putting you through a lifetime of pure hell." He is addressing his wife's family, his daughter, but he does not turn to look at them. It's a decision he made, he tells me later, to spare them. I look at the group. They look weary, wrung out. A few look down at their laps; most stare ahead, their eyes glassy, their expressions blank. The story Michael tells, a story of shame and remorse, of anguish and regret, is powerful. But the other story, the one steeped in pain as raw today as it was three decades ago, a story of violence so vividly remembered as to be truly indelible, is more powerful. Both are true.

—⁓—

Michael's lawyer, the one who has spent a total of one hour getting to know him, launches into his final statement. He calls Michael a "model prisoner"—which is true, but went almost completely unexplored during the hearing. I'm confused about this. In the "Murder & Aggravated Murder Rehabilitation Hearings" worksheet I poured over earlier this week, I noted a ten-item "evidence of rehabilitation" list. Yes, there is actually a list. But, as Steven and four of my guys who have been through the hearing process have told me, the list seems to have little bearing on the proceedings or the decision. There's a list, but proving the potential for rehabilitation is not a matter of checking all the boxes on the list. It's not that transparent. It's not that objective. However, it does seem as if at least some of the items on the list, some of things that speak well of Michael, some of the boxes that might be checked, ought to have touted by the lawyer: Michael's long history of prison employment, the details of his near-spotless institutional disciplinary history, his parole plan, his mental health. But the hearing has focused on only item number six from the list, "the inmate's prior criminal history:" The terrible crime he committed, the horrific action for which he can never make amends. Later, reading ex-con John Irwin's book *Lifers: Seeking Redemption in Prison*, I learn that the major complaint among lifers who have been repeatedly denied parole is that their hearings are not about how they have changed but rather are a retrying of their original offenses.

Obviously the family does not forgive him. But that's not what this hearing is about, is it? Has he spent enough time behind bars to pay for what he did? How can that possibly be measured? Michael has now been in prison longer than his wife was alive. Last week I read a chilling essay in a book of chilling essays (*Hell Is a Very Small Place*) written by prisoners who had spent decades in solitary confinement. One, a man named William Blake, writing in his twenty-ninth year of solitary confinement, wondered if any amount of remorse would matter to a victim, if any level of contrition would be quite enough, or if "endless retribution" was the only answer.

The question for the panel today, as it was in 2012, is, Has Michael changed? Is he a different man from the one who murdered his wife twenty-eight years ago? Does he give evidence of having undergone a fundamental transformation? As members of a parole board, they have to believe in second chances, don't they? Isn't this why they exist? To mete out these chances to the deserving. But do they believe that even the worst of us, the ones who have committed heinous acts, the ones who've stabbed their wives eleven times, that people like *that* deserve a second chance?

The hearing ends. I am left with two competing images, images I will think about for months to come:

One is the scene painted by the Washington County assistant DA: Brenda's mother in her trailer, facing Michael, holding up his toddler, begging him not to do whatever it is he is about to do.

The other is Michael, his meaty shoulders hunched like a wounded bear, his shackled hands reaching for a tissue in his back pocket.

Twenty

I OPEN THE DOOR TO THE ROOM WE MOST OFTEN MEET IN, AND it takes me a moment to register the scene. There, sitting on the aged folding chairs on either side of a long table, are ten men. *Ten.* I think this may be the first time that everyone who might be considered an official part of the group has shown up in the same room at the same time. Don is the loyalist, here since the beginning, almost never missing a session. Eric was also at that first meeting, but his NA responsibilities have kept him from many of our sessions. It's good to see him here again. Jann was part of that original group but disappeared for many months, then came back, then disappeared, now back again, at least for the moment. Michael joined soon thereafter, and except for the months he spent in the infirmary recovering from his hip surgery, he's been a stalwart. Jimmie was also an early member, but he dropped out of sight after the parole board denial. It took him many months to work through and out of deep depression and decide to start coming to the group again. Wil joined a bit later, wary, hesitant—of me, mostly—but he's been coming regularly for more than a year now. Or as regularly as his yoga class and crisis-counselor job allow him to be. Lee joined long ago, detached, silent, but clearly committed to the endeavor and, as I now know from reading his three-part opus, clearly committed to writing as self-knowledge. Sterling is here, an essential member of the group, the "truth-to-power" crusader who sees writing as activism. James, overworked, underrested James who sometimes falls asleep in his chair, is here, pale and heavy lidded. Kaz, Michael's quirky friend, is here. I think, because the group grew slowly, person by person, and because men came and went, appeared and disappeared, I didn't quite realize that we are ten now. I'm not counting on all ten ever showing up at the same time again, but I take a moment to savor the scene in front of me. We made this group. It's taken the better part of two years. That's the blink of an eye for these lifers. But it's a grip of time for me.

I know they come to our sessions because it's something to do, a break in the boredom. I suspect that getting to spend two hours in a room with a woman might be a draw. I'm not fooling myself about that. But I also know it is more. I believe they are here—and that they keep coming back—because they are learning that being the author of your own story is a position of power. Sterling once said, in that way he has of making pronouncement sound like poetry, "My only freedom is expression." When they write, they are writers; they are not prisoners. Less momentous but maybe just as important, we have fun together, as odd as that sounds. Amid the check-ins and the prompts, the out-loud readings and the little teaching lessons, the aha moments and the choked-up moments, we laugh. Looking at the ten of them around the table, I am filled with pleasure that is made more intense by its incongruity. I realize that I like spending time with these guys more than I do with most of my workday colleagues.

Wil gets up and walks over to a small desk in the corner of the room where one of the NA guys has brought in a grease-stained carton of NA goodies: extra cinnamon rolls as big as heads of cabbage, slathered with gooey white icing. Wil tears off a sheet from a roll of brown paper towels sitting on the desk, grabs a pastry, and, looking around the room, seeing everyone watching him—Mr. Healthy, Mr. Yoga—smiles that almost indiscernible Wil smile and says, "I'm celebrating." We all wait for the follow-up. He makes us wait.

"Very good news," he says, cryptically, after a long silence. Wil is the King of Cryptic. Then he fills us in: He says he was just recently allowed to see his oncologist who came down from Seattle. He's allowed one such off-site visit a year. He has money, so he can afford to pay a private doctor. He has, I think, a considerable amount of money, not ill-gotten gains but businesses, investments, other enterprises handled by those outside. Every once in a while, I ever-so-subtly express interest in the details. He not-so-subtly stonewalls me.

I was aware, after overhearing a conversation months ago, that Wil had survived cancer, but I knew no details and was not about to ask. Now Wil tells us all that he had major surgery eight years ago to remove a tumor. He doesn't say where or what kind, but he does say, with what can only be described as pride, that the surgeon found "all kinds of shrapnel in there," patting his nonexistent gut. The shrapnel is the result of his long military (and longer mercenary) career. They got most of the shrapnel, but they weren't able to get all the cancer. "It'll be back," Wil says the surgeon told him in 2009. Wil sits down with his cinnamon roll, looks around the room, knows we're waiting. "The cancer is not growing," he says. "It's not gone, but it's not growing. It hasn't grown."

"That cancer didn't know who it was dealing with," says Michael. Triumphs are few and far between in here. This is one.

Today's prompt is based on a comment Michael made at our last session. The guys had just finished reading aloud from my prompt about the meanings they assigned to the various terms used to describe them—"offender," "prisoner," "inmate," "convict," "adult in custody"—when Michael sighed deeply and said, "Can we please write about something other than life inside?" It's not that this hadn't occurred to me before. I was aware that I had them writing only about prison life and prison experiences. But this was their area of expertise. This was the world they knew, for most of them the *only* world they had known for their entire adult lives.

It was not just the prompts. I had them writing longer pieces about prison life too. For months I'd been encouraging them to work on drafts of stories we could—with hard work—enter into the PEN America Prison Writing contest. And for months I'd been reading drafts. Sterling's story about his time as a hospice volunteer and the friendship he forged with a dying man had gone through four significant revisions. James had worked and reworked his story about a young woman he met when he was first taken into custody and how they had managed to stay in each other's lives. I had persuaded Jimmie that the various shorter pieces he wrote for me about dealing with his parole denial, depression, and "rebirth" would make a powerful story, and he had worked hard on that. I told Jann that his tale of the short-order grill he operated out of his cell was (or could be) a gem and was well worth spending time on. He was reluctant, but I was persuasive. He'd finally handed me a draft. Michael had been working on multiple versions of a story about his sports "career" inside and the lessons he learned. Don had written a story we'd long discussed, and Kaz had presented me with three poems. Last week I'd submitted seven pieces to the contest, saying a little prayer over each envelope, especially the ones with the stories by Sterling and James. I thought those had the best chance. In fact, I thought they were brilliant.

I mailed the envelopes with such pride. I knew, even if the PEN judges could not possibly know, how much thought, how much work, how much heart went into these stories. As I helped them work through multiple revisions, especially with Sterling, James, and Jimmie, I witnessed not just their growth as storytellers but also their growing sense that what they had to say was important, that each of them not only had a distinct voice but that this voice was worth listening to. It may matter to me more than it does to them, but *I want one of my guys to win a PEN Award*. I want it because it is deserved. But more than that, I want it because when someone has been a loser all his life, when someone has been defined as a loser, treated as a loser, called a loser, if that someone is instead told he is a winner . . .

I don't know how to complete that sentence. It seems to me that the meaning and power of such a win could be inestimable. A spark could be ignited. A life could be changed. I think about the effect an individual win could have on the group, could have on future programs, could have, even, on inmates in the general population who've never used writing to try to understand themselves and their world. And I get carried away.

The contest winners won't be announced for many months. I've heard that PEN gets upwards of five thousand submissions. There are two nonfiction categories, essay and memoir, and three winners in each category. That means the chances of any of my guys winning are little better than one in a thousand. I haven't told them that, and I try not to think of it myself. I try to focus only on how good a few of the stories we submitted are, how the stories illuminate both outer and inner lives, how there is both nuance and power in these stories. But I know I need to entertain the possibility—okay, the probability—that none of the seven pieces is recognized. I know disappointment can be a teachable moment. I know there is much to be said for understanding that fame is fleeing and that self-fulfillment endures. I know we can talk about how looking outward for approval, depending on others to tell you what you're worth, is a losing proposition. I could quote that wonderful poem by Marge Piercy that goes, "The real writer is one / who really writes." Obviously I am practicing that speech already. I do not want to have to deliver it.

The PEN submissions had focused on prison life, and our prompts had almost always focused on prison life. It was not just what they knew; it was what they had to teach me. I also worried that if they wrote about anything outside these walls, it would fill them with yearning, would make them sad, or angry, or increase their sense of helplessness. I felt I was protecting them. But maybe it wasn't my place to be protective. Maybe this was just like that other ill-conceived but well-intentioned notion I had when I didn't want to tell them about my travels or write about privacy because I thought it would be depressing for them.

So today I come in with a nothing-to-do-with-prison prompt: "If you could spend an hour with anyone at all, living or dead, who would that be and what would you want to talk about?" It's cliché prompt, I know, but it does get them away from chronicling prison life while not asking them to write about (and I imagine pine for) the past. Just as I am thinking that today will be first time ever that all the guys will sit together and write on the same prompt at the same time, Eric excuses himself to take care of NA business, and James rests his head on his folded arms and falls asleep. I will not wake him. The others write.

Lee reads first. I assume he has written about wanting to meet and converse with Friedrich Nietzsche or Emmanuel Levinas or some philosopher I've never heard of, so when he starts reading about the dinner he imagines enjoying with Ian Anderson, I laugh out loud, from both shock and delight. Ian Anderson is the flautist and lead singer of the British rock band Jethro Tull. Lee, serious, quiet, studious, so self-contained as to be almost unknowable, is a Jethro Tull fan. If he could meet anyone in the world, it would this Scottish-born musician. "Jethro Tull was it for me," he says. I think the others are as surprised as I am. But I am also so happy to be treated to this glimpse behind the wall that Lee has constructed around himself.

Kaz chooses Bruce Lee, which gets laughs and knowing nods. Don goes on knowledgeably and lyrically about Georgia O'Keeffe. I am the only other person in the room who knows who she is. Jann chooses Jesus, but not from a believer standpoint. "I'd ask him," Jann says, delivering the line like a stand-up comedian, "'Hey, what's all this about God being your father?'" To his disappointment, this doesn't get the laugh he expected.

Jimmie writes about his mother, like a good Irish boy should. I listen, amazed that he chose her. He has written about growing up in a violent, abusive, alcohol-soaked environment, a horrific childhood made possible by both father and mother, separately and in collusion. How can he find tenderness in his heart for this woman? Has he forgiven her, or has he just chosen to forget? Jimmie reads, his voice cracking almost imperceptibly. "I'm tearing up," he says. "Look at that, I'm tearing up." Then he laughs.

Sterling is next. He also writes about the woman who raised him, at least for the first decade or so of his life, the woman he called Momma, who was actually his grandmother.

Wil talks about his wife—they had ten years of marriage before his now twenty-six-and-counting years behind bars—and they remain married. This woman stuck by him. This woman can be trusted. That's what he says, writing and speaking about her with detached admiration, as if she were a military comrade.

Michael has waited until last, which is unusual. He starts to read about wanting to meet some baseball player I've never heard of, Bob Uecker, who I learn was a catcher for the Milwaukee Braves in the 1960s. He was apparently also a sportscaster and comedian. I have pretty much tuned out Michael's recitation of Mr. Uecker's career when he abruptly stops reading and takes a deep breath. "I know this whole 'write about something other than prison' thing was my idea, but the truth is, I can't escape my life. I can't escape myself," Michael says. "I started to write about baseball, but really Bob Uecker is not who I want to talk to." Instead, Michael says that if he could meet and talk with anyone at all, living or dead, it would be his victim. Which is to say his wife, the woman he stabbed to death. He can't articulate what he would say. It is so much bigger than remorse, repentance, or shame. There are no words. He hasn't written anything else. He is staring down at his hands. His face is slack with grief. The silence in the room is respectful.

And knowing. It's not just what Michael has said. It's that we've all heard the news. Michael told me just before our session started. The others heard either from Michael or through the ultraefficient prison grapevine: The rehabilitation hearing, the one I attended, did not go his way. The panel said no, once again flopping him, this time for another two years. Without a positive response from the panel, without their ruling that he is, indeed, rehabilitatable, he cannot go before the parole board—even though he is technically eligible for parole. I was hoping this wouldn't be the panel's decision, but I suspected it might be. Michael is more thoughtful than he appeared that day. He is more self-aware and more *interested* in being more self-aware, which I think is even more important. It speaks to his desire to continue to try to be a better man. He's asked me for a list of books about domestic violence, and I'm in the midst of compiling one. Not surprisingly, most are written for victims not perpetrators, but I have found a few that focus on, as two of the subtitles read, "men who batter." If, by reading, he can teach himself more than he has been able to learn (domestic violence programs being unavailable at the prison), if he can understand the murder not as a single horrific act but rather as the culmination of a pattern of control and aggression, if he can own up not just to the crime but to the mind-set, he may have a better chance at his next rehabilitation hearing.

These sessions are sometimes, maybe more often than not, like this one: emotional rollercoasters. One of the guys will read something that is a real gut-wrencher—how he has ceased to trust anyone, how he has forgotten what privacy even means, how shame is a constant companion—and the men will listen and nod, and I will listen and think, How is it possible to live like this? What kind of strength does it take to keep on living like this? As I listen to all these little stories, every two weeks, month after month, I find that my thoughts about what these guys did to get here, the horrible things they did, recede further and further. Instead I think about their inner strength, their resilience, the enormous energy it takes to go on living these constrained, monitored, routinized, militarized, claustrophobic lives. And they don't just slog through. They show up to a writing group or work with PTSD vets or sit in vigil as a hospice volunteer or start a program for at-risk teens or put in double, triple overtime to impress some parole board that may never convene.

I have not gotten used to the emotional wallop of these sessions, and I hope I never do. But sometimes what haunts me when I am not here in this room with these men is not the stories themselves but the trust they have invested in me to hear and learn from these stories, to make something of these stories, to use these stories to shine a light on their hidden lives. These thoughts lead me, at least every other month, to check in with them again about what they are revealing, what they want to reveal. We talk about making the invisible visible, about what people really want to see and what they need to see. Sterling nods, smiling. "Yeah, yeah," he says. "You're helping us write our stories while we're helping you write yours. That feels right."

"Remember, Jimmie, when we were talking about using pseudonyms for all of you, and you said, 'No, go ahead and use my name. You can't do me any more harm than I've done myself.'"

He laughs. "Yeah, that's what I said, and I'll say it again." Then his face changes. He gets serious. "I've got to ask you one thing," he says. "Don't take this wrong." I have no idea what is coming next. "Will you leave us?" he asks. "I mean when you've written what you want to write, will you leave us?"

On one level—and not the most important one—he is asking, in a gentle way, if I am an opportunist. But I also hear the wounded child in him. No one wants to allow himself to feel a connection and then have it severed. No one wants to be left. Before I have a chance to answer, he says, "You know it happens all the time here. People come and people go. You think they're there for you, and then they're not. We're used to it."

I know they are. I know that friends and family vanish over the decades, that prison buddies are paroled, that volunteers come and go. I know that over time, the only people they want to get close to, to count as friends, are fellow lifers. The ones who won't disappear on them. I know I have a responsibility here, and I hope I can live up to it.

I look around the table, catching everyone's eye. "I'm not going any-where," I say.

Twenty-One

JIMMIE HANDS ME A SINGLE SHEET OF PAPER, LINED LOOSE-leaf, filled with his distinctive schoolboy cursive. It's a Christmas poem, he says, written by some con long ago. He doesn't remember when. He doesn't remember who. But he remembers most of the poem, and he's written it out for me from memory. He apologizes that he can't recall the last verse or two. "I just know that they lock 'im up," he tells me. He realizes I have no idea what he's talking about. "Santa, I mean," he says. "You'll see. That's the point of the poem, I guess. Christmas all locked up."

It's just a few weeks before Christmas—the twentieth, thirtieth (or more) holiday season these men have spent in cell blocks. I start to read the poem to myself, but the rest of the guys are now filing into the room for the writing group, so I ask Jimmie if he'll read the poem aloud. He blushes. He is the king of introverts. He thinks that's a bad thing. I've brought in my copy of *Quiet: The Power of Introverts in a World that Can't Stop Talking* for him to read. It has made me proud to be an introvert. "Okay," he says, looking down, "but there might be something offensive in it." The guys know I am unfazed by rough language, salacious humor, or bathroom witticisms.

I steel myself. "Go ahead."

Jimmie begins: "'Twas the night before Christmas / And all through the cells . . .'"

Michael starts laughing. "Oh, yeah, this is a good one," he says.

Jimmie starts again:

'Twas the night before Christmas
And all through the cells,
The convicts were locked up

171

Madder than hell.
Except for the lifers
Kicked back on their bunks
With heads full of visions
Of fat little punks.
Suddenly there arose
A noise from the rooftop.
In marched the goon squad
Ready to hit.
The captain yelled out,
"Who started this shit?"
"It came from the rooftop,"
Sniveled some little bitch.
"It must be a break—
Catch the son of a bitch."
They ran to the rooftop
By the way of the stairs
And found a little freak
In red underwear.
"Ho, ho," said the dude.
"I bring you good cheer."
"I'll be damned," said the captain.
"We caught us a queer."

It seems everyone in the room knows the poem, although, like Jimmie, no one can recite the remaining verses. They're chuckling. "It's the 'queer' part," says Jimmie. "I know that's not right, but that's the poem." He looks to make sure I'm okay with that. His gaze is tentative. Jimmie has a tough-guy face but not the eyes to go with it. I think that's part biology—he has one weak eye and one eye swimming with vitreous floaters—and part learned prison affect. He rarely looks me right in the eye, and when I look at him for too long, he looks down.

"Not great, Jimmie," I say, "but I'll live." Given all the horror stories (some true, some not) about prison rape, given the oft-told jokes-that-are-not-jokes about "bending over to pick up soap in the shower," the fact that Jimmie is sensitive to the poem's insulting use of "queer" is both surprising and heartening.

The poem, Santa's sexual identity notwithstanding, is another example of making lemonade from lemons, of these guys reclaiming at least a bit of what has been taken away in their long confinement. I listen to the animated conversation that follows Jimmie's recitation.

They are talking about the poem, about when they first heard it, about this guy who maybe wrote it, and about Christmases past. When you've spent most of your adult life in one place and you reach a certain age, you reminisce with old friends—even when that life has been spent in prison and your friends are fellow convicts. Out in the free world, we reminisce about when there was free parking downtown, when there was no such thing as hemp milk, when we didn't have to put all our liquids in three-ounce bottles in a quart-sized Ziploc. What do lifers reminisce about? When you could smoke. When there was boxing. When there were trees out in the yard. A friend who got paroled. A friend who died. And Christmases. For those serving a grip of time, prison is not a nasty interlude in their life. It *is* their life. And holidays are part of that life.

I have them write about food for the prompt today. It's a popular topic of conversation, a recurring rant, a running joke. But as a writing exercise, it is (I tell them) a chance to practice their powers of description. "I want to be able to taste what you write about," I tell them.

"Uh, no you don't," says James. Michael snorts. Then they write. It's the expected litany of mystery meat, stringy beans, watery milk, gluey pasta, and cardboard toast. They have fun with it. More fun, I suspect, than they had eating it. I'm glad to hear them laugh. I am glad to give them something light to write about. With the holidays coming, my newsfeed has been full of the usual articles about seasonal stress and depression and about how for many of us the happy holidays are not always happy. I read about what contributes to feeling particularly low at a time when you are supposed to feel particularly joyous, and the list pretty much defines life in prison: inability to be with family and friends, lack of social support, knowledge (or suspicion) that everyone but you is having fun, memories of holidays in the distant past that reflect much happier times, lack of funds. "Cures" include what is not possible for those in prison: Get out into nature! Meet new people! Start new traditions! But I am supposing to know how they handle or celebrate or mourn the holiday season, and really I don't. And so I ask them to write about their "best" or most memorable Christmas inside. I don't want to use this as a prompt. I want them to take their time, so I assign it as homework to be completed by our next session.

"I don't know how memorable this is gonna be," says Michael after I explain the assignment, "but Lifers' Club is having its Christmas party in two weeks. Will you come?" I tell him that I'm delighted with the invitation, but I wonder if I'll have to secure various levels of permission to join them.

"Oh, this one's easy," says Don. "We're allowed to ask a few guests. You just get on the list, and you're in."

—◦◦◦—

Two weeks later, I'm back at the prison for the party. This was not my first Lifers' Club social gathering. I had attended the annual "banquet" (hamburgers, chips, donuts) a while back, flanked by Sterling and Michael, where Kyle, the club's president, had made a big show of presenting me with a printed certificate of appreciation. I suspected Sterling and Michael, who did not seem surprised by the announcement, were behind it. I was touched and misty-eyed, and the only thing that saved me from being a real sap in front of the hundred or so men at the event was the fact that Kyle (or someone) had gotten my last name wrong. So when I walked to the front of the room to get the certificate and pose for a grip 'n' grin for the prison photographer, I looked at the certificate and joked that I was accepting it on the behalf of someone named "Lauren Keller," who apparently was much appreciated.

The most important part of that previous experience was that I was schooled in these two tenets of correct guest etiquette: (1) Take everything that is offered, and (2) Go for seconds. I had botched this by asking for one veggie burger rather than the two hamburgers offered and by declining the chips and saying no to the donuts. Michael was appalled. "I don't eat hamburgers," I told him when I returned to our seating area with my modest plate.

He just looked at me. "But *I* do," he said. "When they call for seconds, take everything." Sterling nodded in agreement. So now I knew.

That banquet had been held in the visiting room, an uninviting space that seemed much smaller than it was because of low ceilings, dim light, and a maze of vinyl chairs and small couches. This Christmas party is being held in the big auditorium-style room—the most expansive space in the prison—that is at the center of the activities floor. This is not, however, a *holiday party* holiday party. There are no decorations. There is no music. There is no guy decked out in a red suit handing out candy canes. The guests are not dressed in their finest. But still, it is a communal event, a break from the routine, a chance to eat food from the outside. So in the context of prison, yes, a party. The big room is set up with long metal tables and folding chairs. At the back of the room, four or five tables have been placed end to end to display and serve the food: stacks of pizza boxes, plastic liter bottles of soda, gallon cartons of ice cream.

I figure the pizza is just about room temperature. I helped bring it into the prison close to an hour ago. When I arrived late this afternoon to be processed and scanned, Steven was standing just inside the entrance, carefully transferring stacks of pizza boxes from delivery pallets into what looked like laundry carts that could be wheeled into the prison. I lent a hand. The grease stains were just blooming. The boxes were hot then. Not so much now. Regardless, pizza is clearly a big draw. The room is noisy and crowded. It smells like a pepperoni factory. I'm not sure if this is the only holiday party—I know other clubs are allowed to plan and schedule events—but the Lifers' Club is one of the biggest, best organized, and best (self-)funded clubs in here. This may be the only game in town this season.

It used to be, back in the days when my guys first got here, that the prison made what they remember as a real effort around holiday time. On Christmas Eve, each prisoner got two cans of soda and a brown paper sack of fresh-popped popcorn. That evening they could stay up late watching movies in the television room. It was a big deal. Christmas dinner the next day was, as Jimmie had told me, a "fat slice of ham" and a "real slice of turkey." But those days are long gone. The Christmas Eve treat is now an apple, an orange, and a prison-made cookie. No one gets to stay up late. For Christmas dinner, Jimmie says he hasn't seen a slice of ham in "at least a decade" and that the pressed turkey they now get for dinner "had no father or mother." That makes this evening's event even more special.

I walk into the big room and nod at the CO sitting behind the desk, the man who makes sure each prisoner scans his ID card as he enters so the system knows where everyone is. We recognize each other and exchange a smile. There are some good people who work here, and he is one of them. I've seen how he interacts with the guys as they come and go. He treats them as individuals. I look around, scanning the sea of blue—dark-blue T-shirts, dark-blue sweatshirts, prison jeans—until I spot Michael at the far end of the room. He sees me at the same time and raises his arm. He's secured a table near the perimeter of the room. I am betting it is as close as he could get to the food line. Don, Lee, Jimmie, and Sterling are already seated. James, I am told, is working overtime again. Wil might be with a client. I ask about Eric and Jann, but no one knows where they might be. We all sit, chatting about not much of anything, waiting for the food line to be called. If I weren't in a maximum-security prison on a heavily guarded floor sharing a table with convicted murderers, I'd liken this experience to my high school cafeteria days: the smell of food teetering on the border between savory and nauseating, the noise, the high spirits, the visible cliques, the mix of "popular" tables (of which I believe we are one) and outcasts.

The line is called, with guests given first preference. Michael gives me a look. "Get up there," he says, reminding me, in case I've forgotten, to say yes to everything. I have not forgotten. I come back to the table with a paper plate sagging under the weight of three enormous slices of pizza and a paper bowl mounded with several scoops of vanilla ice cream liberally laced with chocolate syrup. I enjoy being Lady Bountiful with the pizza, but the ice cream is all mine. Michael interrupts my ice cream feed to tell me that there are a few guys who would like to meet me. Is that okay? He signals to someone at the table behind us, and a middle-aged man ambles up. "This is our teacher," Michael says, introducing me. The guy extends a calloused hand, and I shake it. He wants to know if I'll look at some writing he's done. I say yes. Another guy comes by. Another introduction. Then Michael says there's a guy who wants to meet me, but he doesn't walk so well, isn't feeling so good. Would I mind walking over to his table? It would surprise people—it surprised me—how many prisoners walk with canes or push walkers. That's what happens when you put people away for three or more decades in a place that promotes premature aging, especially if those people didn't come in all that healthy to begin with. We walk across the room. I feel both conspicuous and pro-tected. Michael is enjoying his self-appointed role as host. I am enjoying the credibility my connection to Michael and the others confers on me. I shake another hand, field another inquiry about looking at writing. Then it's back to the table, back up to the line for seconds, back with the guys to dole out more pizza and just, well, hang out.

—⁓—

A few days later I am at the prison again, this time for our last session of the year. Steven has worked one of his miracles and secured permission, for the second time, for me to bring in a box of baked goods, my holiday gift to the men. I would have loved to bring in something home baked, but that is absolutely verboten. Steven shakes his head and laughs when I mention it. So these treats are from a small bakery in town, one of those places where every item is a little work of art. I open the box and place it in the middle of the table. We all spend a quiet moment admiring the little cakes and cookies. Then I grab the box and pass it to my left to James, who is sitting next to me. James shakes his head and passes it across the table to Wil. Wil makes his choice, and the box is passed to Don, Jimmie, then Michael. The elders. The younger men (James, Sterling, Lee) defer to them, showing their respect. They do so without fanfare, without comment. There is such grace in this moment, such kindness.

"Today I want to hear what you wrote about Christmases past," I say. "You're all veteran storytellers now, so my expectations are high."

I'm teasing them a little, but Jimmie looks up, worried. "Uh-oh," he says. Everyone laughs.

Well, Wil doesn't actually laugh, but his eyes crinkle, indicating mild amusement. "I don't celebrate Christmas or any holiday," he says, not Scrooge-like but emphatic. "But I'm interested. I'll listen."

James didn't have time to do the assignment. He continues to work any overtime that's offered, and in the commercial laundry, there is always overtime. Kaz admits he forgot. Assigning a writing exercise as homework has the benefit of giving them more time to develop their ideas and practice some of the writing lessons I casually introduce. But it also means, unlike with the in-class prompt, not everyone does the writing. There's work, visits, other club responsibilities, readings for a college class. I actually appreciate it when those who don't have time to do a thoughtful job don't just write something. I interpret it as a sign that they take their writing seriously and that they respect the group.

Jimmie has written almost seven pages. His piece is entitled "Best Christmas in Three Decades of Incarceration" and focuses on 2004, the year he met and married Donna and "celled up" with her son Robby. Until then Christmases had been getting increasingly more depressing. The cards and letters he used to get from family—he writes that he used to decorate a wall of his cell with them—had stopped coming. That's what happens when you're in for as long as Jimmie, as long as the other men. Your parents die. Your siblings move on with their lives. Your friends make new friends. Some people just want to forget you ever existed, and as the years go by, they do. What Jimmie got for Christmas was a card from the Salvation Army. He was grateful for that. But it also reminded him of what he had lost.

Then, in 2004, his life began again. Donna and her son were Christmas enthusiasts, and he felt himself being pulled into what he had forgotten was the spirit of the season. Donna started sending in sheets of Christmas wrapping paper and magazine pages illustrated with ornaments and decorations. Jimmie and Robby cut out the pictures of the ornaments and taped them to their cell walls. They hung them from their book shelf. Jimmie made a tree out of pages torn from a *National Geographic* magazine. They used the paper Donna sent in to wrap little gifts, mostly purchased from the commissary—candy, soup, socks—and placed the packages under their handmade, magazine-scrap tree. "Hands down, we had the most decorated cell the Oregon State Penitentiary has ever seen," Jimmie writes. He adds a thank you to OSP for allowing this back then. "In no other joint in the state could we have done this." I have heard variations on this theme from almost all the men during the last two years. OSP is the state's only maximum-security prison, but inmates who have spent time in other facilities in the state think kindly—if that's a word that can be used in this context—of this place. It is less militarized, they say. It is more humane.

On that Christmas morning in 2004, Jimmie and Robby awoke early. Jimmie writes that he stood at the front of his cell impatiently waiting for the doors on the tier to slide open. When they did, he positioned himself in front of his cell, watching as the other inmates began to file by. He remembers that their heads were down. No one was talking. The mood was grim. "Hey, man, Merry Christmas," Jimmie called out to a guy he didn't know who was passing by the cell. The guy acknowledged the greeting, then looked down, kept walking. Jimmie called out again, inviting him to come into his cell and get a present from under the tree. The guy thought Jimmie was playing a joke on him. Or worse. He entered the cell slowly, warily. Then, seeing there actually was this little tree and there actually were little wrapped packages under it, he chose one. And so did fifteen other men that morning. Jimmie writes that whatever look they had on their faces when they came in the cell, it wasn't the same look they had when they left. He and Robby had, he writes, "changed their lives for a day."

Sterling begins his "most memorable Christmas" story this way: "A Rabbi, Buddhist Minister and Christian preacher sitting down for lunch with three prisoners seems like it would be the beginning of a joke, but for me it was my favorite Christmas in prison." I laugh when I hear this. I remember thinking the very same thing, reciting a joke line in my head, when I sat in one of my training sessions along with a rabbi, an imam, and an Evangelical. The three prisoners are Sterling, a North Dakota Indian, and a six-foot-seven, 285-pound Paul Bunyan look-alike known for being a two-time winner of the prison's eating contest (thirty hot dogs and two pies in less than five minutes). Prison is such an unremittingly harsh place. We read about gangs and gang violence, race wars behind bars. And here is a story about a half-black, half-Italian guy (that's Sterling, who calls himself a "marvelous mulatto"), an American Indian, and a huge white guy—all of whom serve as chapel clerks—eating a peaceful holiday meal with a Jew, a Buddhist, and a born-again. I am trying (and failing) to imagine this happening in the free world. They eat sushi. Sterling thinks about the sixty-four different religious denominations or spiritual practices, the services and classes and events, that are part of the culture in the prison. He doesn't much like sushi—"Ain't this raw fish?" he asks—but he clearly likes the company. This is a favorite Christmas memory.

Michael's story is an epic. It is overlong (eighteen handwritten pages), and it wanders, but it is some of the best writing he has ever done. It tells a story that is quintessentially Michael, which means it is funny, slightly smart-ass, and more than slightly food obsessed. But it is also charming, tender, heartwarming, and not really what you would expect from this bear of a man. I have to navigate through a labyrinthine plot, but here is the essence: Michael's Christmas story is two stories, both of which take place at a Lifers' Club holiday party some years back. The first is about this "youngster," Billy, who was "alright" because he had "good paper work" (that is, he was neither a sex offender nor a snitch), who attached himself to Michael and his buddy Randy as they were making their way up to the activities floor for the party. Billy was a short-timer doing only forty months. Lifers rarely paid attention to short-timers, but Billy reminded Michael of himself back in the day, so he let him tag along. The thing was, Billy was not a lifer and thus was not eligible to attend the club party. Somehow the kid managed to get through the ID scan, but when it came to getting pizza on the line, the lifer doling out the food shook his head.

"You're not on the list," he told Billy. It was a list of those in the Lifers' Club. Michael pulled out a couple of soda coupons from his pocket. They are used as currency inside. He palmed the coupons and extended his hand in a money handshake, but the guy shook his head again, refused. "Can't," he said. "We're short already."

Michael reached back across the serving table again and gave him the handshake anyway. "Happy holidays," he said. Giving without the expectation of receiving. Now there's a concept. Back at the table, Michael gave Billy a slice of pizza from his own plate, which for Michael was a sacrifice to end all sacrifices.

The other story, intertwined with the ongoing Billy-the-interloper tale, is the saga of Michael searching for those little packets of crushed red-pepper flakes that come with delivered pizza. He is intent on find-ing a stash of them somewhere—after all, dozens and dozens of pizza boxes were delivered—not so that he can spice up his pizza at the party (pizza was enough of a treat by itself, he writes) but because he could use them to season the bland mainline food for weeks and months to come. Michael asks the guys behind the serving line. He prowls the floor. He looks in drawers and cubby holes. He goes into the Lifers' Club cage and rifles through the desk. Nothing.

The two stories come together at the end when Michael, on his way back to the table, is stopped by one of the guys who had been behind the serving line, the guy with the clipboard who didn't see Billy's name on the list. The guy is holding out a tray with several pieces of pizza, extras. "Here," he says, handing Michael the tray. "Merry Christmas." The pizza is for Billy. Michael sits down, gives all but one slice of pizza to Billy, then picks up the last slice of pizza for himself.

"You eating pizza like that?" Randy asks.

"Like what?" says Michael.

Then Randy pulls several dozen packets of crushed red-pepper flakes from his pocket and hands them over. "You'll probably need some of these," he says, deadpan. Michael looks up and sees the "don't even ask" expression on Randy's face.

The last line of the story is Michael's. "Damn," he says. "There really is a Santa."

It's irresistible, this double tale of generosity and friendship. Add to that Sterling's simple scene of cross-cultural, interracial, interdenominational camaraderie and Jimmie's almost allegorical "random acts of kindness" account. It seems to me that these are not just windows into the way life is lived behind bars, not just hints that decent and meaningful lives can (and are being) led. They are tales of rehabilitation and redemption. They are true Christmas stories.

Twenty-Two

MOST PEOPLE WHO GO TO PRISON ARE EVENTUALLY RELEASED. They do their time. They get out. They make a life for themselves. Or they don't. They commit another crime or they violate parole. And they're back, paperwork in hand, gates clanging behind them, sentenced for another stretch. Statistics are not people, but statistics tell a story too. The Bureau of Justice Statistics reports that "at least 95 percent of all state prisoners" are released "at some point." Of these, about one-quarter are "violent offenders." But that's a big category that can include assault, rape, kidnapping, robbery, manslaughter, and extortion in addition to murder. All of the men in the writing group except Eric are convicted murderers (Eric's crime was vehicular homicide), and the release of these "violent offenders" is a different story. One Stanford study found that lifers had an 18 percent chance of being released. Another that tracked the fate of lifers between 1990 and 2010 found that a murderer had a 6 percent chance of leaving prison alive.

And yet other statistics very much favor the granting of parole to those who've committed murder. A study of California lifers convicted of homicide and later paroled found that fewer than 1 percent returned to jail. As the Harvard researcher Marieke Liem put it in her thoughtful book, *After Life Imprisonment*, "contrary to popular perception, older offenders who have committed homicides are the least likely of all offenders to recidivate." "Recidivate" means to commit another crime and end up in jail again. The five-year-out recidivism rate for all prisoners, based on Bureau of Justice Statistics findings, is 76.6 percent.

Of my writers, who has a chance of leaving prison? Not Lee. He was sentenced to thirty-six years plus, when that stretch is over in 2032, *five* life without parole sentences. Maybe not Sterling. He has a de facto life without parole sentence, meaning he wasn't actually sentenced to life *without* parole, but rather he was sentenced to several life *with* parole sentences to be served consecutively, which ends up being the same thing. He is in the midst—and has been in the midst for years—of battling this in court, given that he was a minor when convicted and that the Supreme Court ruled in 2012 that mandatory life without parole sentences for juveniles are unconstitutional. Of course, his is a de facto life without sentence, not a "legal" (and no longer constitutional) sentence, so it is unclear if he will win this battle.

The other guys are serving life with the possibility of parole, emphasis on the word "possibility." That doesn't mean probability. It means maybe. It means there might be a chance. State sentencing laws have changed over the years, including the passage of a mandatory sentencing measure in the mid-1990s and, before that, the creation of a matrix that codified crime and punishment. Some of the guys fell before the matrix system existed, like Don, who has been behind bars since 1985. Others are matrixed, which means they fall under different guidelines. But in general a life with the possibility of parole sentence means that after twenty-two years, or maybe twenty-five years, or possibly thirty years, a lifer could be eligible for release. The rehab panel has to find him rehabilitatable. Then the parole board, in a separate decision, has to find the prisoner worthy of parole.

Wil, at seventy-nine, is convinced he will die in prison. When I asked him more than a year ago if he'd ever appeared before a rehabilitation panel or a parole board, he said he had and that "they said no, and they told me never to come back." I didn't go to his hearing nor did I ask for details—Wil gives details when Wil wants to give details—but it is easy to imagine, now that I've sat through Michael's hearing, how Wil would have played before a review panel: the stoicism, the icy glare, the clipped delivery of just the essentials, the sense that you are in the presence of someone who knows who he is and doesn't care what you think about it. The panel wants to see shame and guilt and remorse. Wil owns his actions (and by that I mean his crimes), but he does not look backward.

His Zen training and meditation have brought him to a place of detachment and in-the-now living. The implacability of that, the chilly calmness of that place, would send just the wrong message to those reviewing his case. But there is so much more to Wil, as I have learned, as he has ever so slowly let me see: his extraordinary empathy for those in distress, his deep-banked energy, his lion heart. On the other hand—and he would probably be the first to say this—if released and if faced with a fight-or-flight situation, he would fight. And, his age notwithstanding, I bet he would win. So maybe the panel was right.

And then there's Jann, who has already served more than thirty-five years of a life with the possibility of parole sentence, who has, he told me, participated in forty-two different self-help, self-improvement, anger management, and education programs, who has been denied eight times at the rehabilitation hearing level. After he told me this, anger in his voice, he was silent for a long minute, looking down, clearly, it seemed to me at the time, controlling the urge to cry. "What do I have to do?" he said finally, looking up, eyes bloodshot. "I don't know any more." I don't know either. The inner workings of the review panels, the inner thoughts of those who sit on them can be—are—opaque.

Jimmie, also with the possibility of parole, has been denied twice. It was that last denial he wrote about, the one that drove him deep into depression, the one that he said eventually "freed" him to live his own life. It may be that the authentic life he is now trying to embrace will be lived out entirely behind bars. After the long buildup and the high hopes and the grand plans that buoyed him, after the reverberating shock of the denial, he may not have it in him to try a third time. Michael, denied twice, will try again in two years. If he can show the board what I know is in him, if he can learn the vocabulary to express what he feels and what the board needs to know he feels, maybe he will be deemed rehabilitatable and be allowed to go before the full parole board. And maybe the board will say yes.

There is hope for James, the youngest in the group, who has spent all of his twenties and now just about all of his thirties behind bars. He can make his case before the rehabilitation panel in 2021. His over-the-top work ethic will impress the panel, and he is as clean-cut as they come. His relative youth will give the panel hope that he can start a new life. He might, in his early forties, have a shot at a job, even a family. I know this sounds cruel, but the panel will also like how heavy the burden of his crime weighs on him. He once wrote, in response to a prompt, "I am crippled by shame. I am a murderer. I will always be a murderer."

Don, the optimist against all odds, the guy who has successfully worked through six five-year self-improvement plans, sees himself released in 2026. It is possible. Kaz, because he came in more recently under other sentencing guidelines, knows he will be released in 2024.

That leaves Eric, the only one in the group who has made parole. He will be released in just a few months after serving—for this, his third stretch in prison—twenty-two years. Do not imagine the Hollywood movie release-from-prison scene. Eric will not stride out of the gate, grinning, dressed in civilian clothes carrying a plastic bag with his worldly goods. He will not be met by his weary-but-loyal wife or his best buddy in a beater car. Eric will be escorted out by guards, cuffed and dressed in prison blues, placed in a Department of Corrections transport van and driven to the county jail, where he will spend as much as another year before his final release.

—ɯ—

Is there such a thing as a Hollywood-style release-from-prison moment? I had witnessed a modified version a few years back when Belinda, a prisoner at Coffee Creek Correctional Facility, was paroled after spending twenty-two years inside. At eighteen, she'd been convicting of stabbing her pimp. She hadn't meant to kill him, she told me, just hurt him. I had spent a few hours with her during the month before her release, thinking I might write a "what happens after you leave" story. She allowed me to witness the morning of her release. I stood outside the gate, in the rain, fifteen feet away, watching. She came out wearing sweat pants a size too large and a cheap rain jacket, clothes brought in by a friend the day before. She was lit up, like a girl rushing out to meet her prom date. There was no prom date. There was a clutch of late-middle-aged women from a faith-based group who had connected with her in prison. There was a dog. It was one of the dogs she had helped train as part of a prison-run canine companions program. She briefly hugged the women, then got down on one knee and nuzzled the dog for a long moment. The dog remembered her.

The ladies knew exactly where Belinda wanted to go. They had obviously discussed this moment. In two cars, they caravanned to the nearest Starbucks, which was less than two minutes away. Belinda hesitated at the door, waiting for two of the ladies to go in first. They found a table. They ordered for her. She wanted a caramel Frappuccino. I watched her take that first sip. A month later, we met for dinner at a local steakhouse, where she ordered the most expensive item on the menu, ignored me completely, and texted nonstop during the entire meal. She had gotten a phone three weeks before. She had acquired a boyfriend two weeks before. At forty, she was a teenager.

I also knew something about Trevor's release. Trevor had been the president of the Lifers' Club when I first came to OSP. It was he who first introduced me at a club function when I was trolling for members for my yet-to-happen writers' group. He was serving a life sentence, convicted at age fourteen for the murder (with his older brother) of one of the pillars of his small rural community. It had been a notorious crime. His release, sixteen years later, was contentious and controversial. He had qualified for early release under Oregon's "second look," a 2015 statute that allowed people convicted as minors to have the chance to get out of jail after serving half their sentence. Trevor was a great candidate. He had spent his years in prison amassing an extraordinary record of education, rehabilitation, and accomplishment. Character witnesses lined up to testify on his behalf. After spending not just half of his sentence but half of his life behind bars, Trevor was granted parole. When I arranged to meet him and his fiancée at a local Denny's, he had been out for more than two years, but there were parts of the case still pending. In fact, he had just come from a legal hearing. I wanted to know about that morning he was released, that first day, that first week. I might not get to experience this with any of the men in my writers' group. It was such an important, such an earth-shaking, life-changing moment. I wanted to learn all I could about it. Fresh from yet another legal encounter, Trevor was glad to talk about something else.

That day, the morning of his release, Trevor didn't stride out the front gate into the waiting arms of friends and family. He went out in shackles, accompanied by his parole officer with two guards flanking him. They drove directly to the local parole and probation office, where he was outfitted with an ankle monitor. Then his parole officer drove him to his mother's house. He remembers walking slowly through the whole house, inspecting every room, looking in every closet, opening every cupboard. It wasn't paranoia. It was intense curiosity. There was so much stuff. So much *different* stuff. His first meal was takeout sub sandwiches. He'd wanted to go out, but there was a cop car parked out front, and he knew they'd be tailed. For dinner, his mother made his favorite meal, pot roast. On day two he threw up. "Nerves," he told me. Then he went to the DMV to take his written test for a driver's permit. Then to Ross Dress for Less for some clothes. On day three he tried sushi for the first time. A few days later he got permission from his parole officer to go to the coast, where he and his girlfriend stood on the beach and stared at the horizon.

I listen to him recount all this, hungry for details. It seems to me that Trevor's transition back to the free world was remarkably smooth. He credits his mother, his girlfriend. He has a place to live. He has marketable skills. He is only thirty-one. He can start a life. I know it will be different, very different, for Eric when he gets out.

—⚓—

It's a surprise when Eric shows up to the writers' group one afternoon not to tell me he has a conflict, not to apologize for his absences, not to drop off a piece of writing and leave, but to sit down with the rest of the guys, to write and talk.

"I'm a two-digit midget," he says, pulling up a chair and allowing himself a little smile. That means, in prison slang, that he is less than a hundred days away from release. Then he looks down and says no more. He knows two of the men in the room will never leave prison. He knows others have a chance, but that chance is years down the road. He wishes he could talk about his release, but it would be insensitive and disrespectful. Instead he hands me a rambling eight-page handwritten note. I had asked him, several times during the past few months, to write about how he was preparing for this release.

"Wow. I am scared shitless." That's how he begins. "It doesn't seem real." It doesn't seem real even though Eric has been working on making this day happen for the past twenty-plus years. This is his third stretch—he started serving time in 1988—and he has been determined to make it his last. He'd ruined too much—his marriage, his family, the woman he killed in the collision and her family. This time he would make big changes that would stick, the biggest one being staying away from drugs. Meth had taken over and ruined his life. In prison, two decades of NA had helped him, he wrote, "become free even when incarcerated."

Back when he started this stretch, he was devoted to a woman named Tara. He referred to her as "my common law wife." He wrote about their tumultuous relationship, the children she bore from different fathers while he was in prison, her addiction, recovery, relapse, her time in jail. He thought of her children as his. He sent her money, most of the money he made at his prison job plus the money he made crafting jewelry in the prison hobby shop. Then, in the midst of his planning for their future, when he finally got a release date, he found out she had married someone. He was stunned (although maybe he shouldn't have been, given her history). He was shaken. Most of all, he was deeply, deeply wounded. He loved her.

What faces him now, what scares him now, is not just the usual uncertainty of a man being released after essentially three decades of incarceration: the uphill climb as he searches for a job as a three-time-loser felon, a recovering drug addict, a man in his late fifties who has not been in the labor force since the mid-1990s; the daily struggle to stay clean; the reentry into an almost unrecognizable world. What faces him now is the basic uncertainty of daily life. Where will he live? Where can he afford to live? Who will rent him an apartment? The plan for years had been to live with Tara, to be a father to her various fatherless children. That future is gone. And from what I have read about the troubled relationships between women and newly released men, this might not be a bad thing. First, of course, is the fact that she is an addict, and this, regardless of anything else, would have made Eric's continuing recovery even harder than it will already be. There would be the stress of moving into full-time fatherhood; the tightrope of parole and how, for example, a verbal altercation with Tara could be seen as (or reported as) a parole violation. Maybe I have read too much about how parolees can get into trouble, some of it of their own making, some of it the result of unhappy unions, discordant relationships. Something happens—not a crime but an outburst, bad behavior, and the parole officer is called, and the guy goes back inside. With Tara's long-term drug addiction and her unstable and transitory relationships with the various fathers of her children, it could be an accident waiting to happen. I don't know if Eric sees that. Or even if some part of him is relieved that he won't be leaving prison to make a life with Tara. But I do know that he has forced himself to accept what has happened. "I am clean, sober, educated, motivated, and focused on a new life," he writes in a second long note he hands me the day he makes it to the writers' group.

He writes about the emotional support he has gotten from "my friends and brothers" while in prison. "We changed our lives together" is how he puts it. In his note to me, he lists more than thirty people: extended family, former cellies, NA compatriots, people in the recovery community outside. He needs to name them, to acknowledge them not just because he understands the debt he owes those who believe in him but also because he needs to persuade himself that even though Tara and those kids he thought of as his own are not what he's coming home to, he is coming home to something.

He had been scared, he writes, of leaving prison "broke and alone." With the support of friends, he doesn't feel so alone. When the relationship ended with Tara, he started seriously saving money rather than sending it all to her. He opened a credit union account. He took out a small loan and began making payments to establish credit. He established a business account for his jewelry making with the help of an old cellie now on the outside. And he writes about all kinds of entrepreneurial plans: a fencing business (enclosures, not stolen property), a trucking concern, flipping houses. He wants to go back to school to become a counselor or mentor. He has so many ideas. He writes and writes, writing himself out of a place of fear and into a place of hope. At the end of all these cramped, handwritten pages, this is his final sentence: "Writing this right now I realize that I am alright."

I think he will be. I hope he will be. I will not be able to talk to him, or correspond directly in any way, after he leaves OSP. It's one of the restrictions that goes along with my official volunteer status, my precious scannable ID card: no contact with prisoners except during the sponsored activity within these walls. I hope to gather intel from the men in the group. Eric promises to keep in touch this way.

I know about some of the other obstacles he will face, the ones that underlie the daily living challenges he already acknowledges. Harvard's Marieke Liem wrote about what she (and other researchers) considers the biggest hurdle: to unlearn what you learned in prison, to unmake your "institutional self." That self gave up liberty, autonomy, relationships, possessions. That self learned to minimize expectations, to respond to problems as they occur rather than to organize behavior to avoid problems, to present a "prison mask" that suppressed outward signs of emotion, to stand fast in social encounters. No compromise. Compromise is weakness. That self learned to trust no one, to depend on external rewards not internal motivation. That self learned to live with a pervasive sense of disempowerment, the helplessness one learns, over time, when there is little control over one's life. These are coping strategies that work in prison. They are ill suited, counterproductive, unhealthy, and maybe even dangerous in the free world.

A while back, I gave the guys a "before and after" prompt, asking them to describe themselves, to list character traits, before they fell and now. I expected—and mostly got—"angry, out of control, irresponsible" and other negative traits for their preincarceration selves and "respectful, sensitive" and other positives for how they see their prosocial, rehabilitated selves. But Kaz had a different take. He described his free-world self as "self-assured, self-reliant, secure" and his jailed self as "passive, fearful, fractured and insecure." What will face Kaz when he gets out in 2024, after this stretch of twenty-one years, what faces Eric, what will face any long-incarcerated prisoner on release, is the enormous task of relearning to be a human being.

The societal context for this relearning is not a supportive one. There is the stigma of incarceration. This is not just what others think of Eric or Kaz or James or how they treat them but also what these men think of themselves. There is the double whammy of having others view you through the dark lens of "felon," and your own greatly diminished sense of self-worth. The people who might understand what you're going through are exactly the people you cannot associate with. It is a violation of parole to have ex-con friends. There are also the challenges of what researchers have dubbed "desynchronicity," meaning being out of step with your age cohort. Suppose James is released in his early forties or Sterling wins his various appeals and makes it out by his mid-to-late forties. Their age cohort is long married (or married, divorced, remarried). They are fathers. They've been in the workforce for two decades or more. They have acquired the various trappings of middle-aged life. But, when (if) these guys who've served a grip of time reenter the world, they are at a disconcertingly different time in their lives. And the longer the time spent in prison, the more out of step, the more asynchronous, the person. Belinda, released into the world as a forty-year-old woman, texts like a sixteen-year-old to her instant boyfriend.

But maybe Eric will make it. Maybe, despite all the obstacles he faces, all the challenges he knows about and the ones he doesn't, he will stay clean. He will find satisfying and healthy relationships. He will learn how to live a decent life. Reading about what sociologists and others believe makes for success on release from a long stretch in prison, I am heartened. Eric has created, like others who have been successful on the outside, what researchers call a "prototype reform story." He sees himself, at his core, as a "normal" person. His criminal past was a result of bad choices, a cavalcade of bad choices, of failures of conscience, of his inability to act responsibly. If he saw himself instead as the victim, if he blamed others for his fall, his success could be limited. Just as important, he sees himself as changed, as, in his words, "restored and transformed." He believes his life has meaning, which is also a core component of successful reintegration. Through his own personal work, and through his deep belief in NA, he has adopted an "if you know, you owe" mantra that will set him on a path of helping and mentoring others. But perhaps the single most important predictor of success goes back to the unlearning of the institutionalized self. Eric must believe in his own power, his own agency, his ability to succeed. In prison for three stretches that span thirty years, the whole of his middle life, Eric will—after his tacked-on sentence in county jail—enter a world he knows little about. What he learned, and what he has to unlearn, will determine whether two years from now I'll see him walk into this room up on an activities floor and rejoin the writers' group.

I hope to hell I don't.

Twenty-Three

STORIES ARE SUPPOSED TO HAVE ENDINGS. THIS ONE doesn't—or at least not the swelling-of-music, happily-ever-after kind.

It may be that, against the odds, after his imminent release from OSP and a year of step-down at a county jail, Eric makes it. But that is the beginning of his story, not the end. It may be that, two years from now, Michael aces his third attempt with the rehab panel, manages to get before a sympathetic parole board, and wins his release. It may be that, at some time in the unknowable future, Sterling's complicated case finds a receptive judicial ear and that the sixteen-year-old boy who came here leaves as a man well into his forties. I have imagined happy endings, but I have yet to see one. The story of life in prison sometimes ends only when life ends. The end of Wil's story, Wil who just turned eighty this month, the end of Lee's story, will be their deaths behind these walls.

I asked the men in the group how they would feel about writing something for this final chapter. After almost three years of awakening to the power of the written word in their lives—the power of stories in their lives—their voices are strong. I wanted those voices to be the last ones you heard. I wanted them to write the coda to this story with no end.

They were excited. And nervous. One afternoon not long ago, they sat around the table in our usual room, their heads bent over their work, writing on this prompt: *What do you want readers to know about you and your life?* Here is what they wrote:

> We are humans who daily rise above the words used to define us. We live, breath, hope and dream, daily striving to be better human beings. We have real lives, lives of work and play.
>
> —Jimmie

Know that in this realm ruled by negativity, the struggle to keep from being overcome by it is still being fought and won by some.

—Kaz

The only way for these decades to not be in vain is if I can survive. The meaning of my life, as long as this punishment persists, can only be survival.

—Lee

I have aged out of marriage, children, grandchildren, career-building, retirement savings or acquiring a lifetime of good works. But I have made something of myself in here, year by year, decade by decade.

—Don

I was seventeen years old when the front gate to the adult penitentiary closed behind me. I'm now twenty-two years into a life sentence, and although I've grown and matured and developed, in many ways I am still that teenager devastated by the permanence of my actions. I deserve to be here. I understand that. I just want people to know that I am sorry for what I did. I wish I could take it back.

—James

I hope not to be judged by the worst decisions of my life but rather by the man I have become today. Prison can be a warehouse that breeds criminality. Prison can be an opportunity for transformation. Some transform themselves and help transform others, and never get a chance to leave. I have a chance to leave.

—Eric

The last word should be about our victims. I can't speak for everyone, but I can speak about the pain and remorse that each of us felt and shared through our writings. The want and need to redeem ourselves or pay back for what we have done is with us all the time. How do you repay for a life taken? You don't. You can't. But you can live for and honor your victims by being the best person you can be from this day forward.

—Michael

Watch me soar
Even in my chains
Watch me soar
Way above the shame
Watch me soar
Even through the pain
Watch me end the struggle and build forever . . .
Some sit in the dark speaking anger

While others illuminate the night speaking love
Who you gonna be?

—Sterling (from a longer poem)

No book ends on the last page.
No book begins on the first page.
No last, no first—only the page being read.

—Wil

The Lifers' Club writers' group is also a story without an end.
At least I hope so.

Epilogue

SEVEN MONTHS AFTER SENDING IN THE SUBMISSIONS TO THE PEN America Prison Writing Contest, we get the news. Out of the more than five thousand entries received, James's story about his friendship with Sophia wins first-place prize in the memoir category. Sterling's story about sitting with Gus in prison hospice wins second-place prize in the essay category.

Six months later, in the first event of its kind at OSP, James, Sterling, Michael, Lee, Don, Kaz, Wil, and Jimmie read from their work to a group of family and friends in the prison's visitors' room.

The group continues to meet twice a month.

Acknowledgments

WRITING ABOUT PRISONS AND THE LIFE LIVED WITHIN THEIR walls depends first on access and then on trust, neither of which is easily granted. I get that. I get why it is easier to say no than to say yes. And before I found the people who said yes, I spent close to three years seeking out, attempting to cultivate, corresponding with, meeting, pitching, and repitching to many who said no. In that long process, Elizabeth A. Craig, head of the Oregon Department of Corrections (DOC) Office of Communications, lent her help and guidance. My thanks also to Joe Giblin, Elaine Shaw, and Tonya M. Gushard at the DOC for their early efforts on my behalf. Michele McCormack of Chemeketa Community College, with her tireless enthusiasm; Michelle Inderbitzen of Oregon State University, with her clear-eyed compassion; Melissa Buis Michaux of Willamette University, with her vision of restorative justice; and Steven Shankman and Shaul Cohen of University of Oregon, who created and nurture Oregon State Penitentiary's Inside Out program have all, with their integrity, hard work, and success, made my work possible. I owe them deep thanks.

The Lifers' Club writing group owes its existence—this book owes its existence—to the optimism, energy, and tenacious support of one of the biggest yea-sayers I have had the pleasure to meet, Steven Finster, a recreation specialist at Oregon State Penitentiary (OSP). He put forth our proposals, argued for us at staff meetings, kept the channels of communication open, found a place for us on the calendar, was the brains behind the creation of the writing group's lifers' book repository, helped me obtain my official ID, and through it all weathered the usual and unusual storms of bureaucracy with the persistence and strength of the navy vet he is. His boss at the time, Amy Pinkley-Wernz, said yes more than no, which made all the difference. (Her kindness toward Jimmie, I hope she knows, changed his life.) Activities colleague Patrice Lans not only took up the slack during Steven's absence but also spearheaded an extraordinary inmate-initiated project for a healing garden inside the walls. CO Cory Carter belied all the stereotypes you've read about or seen of uncaring (or worse, abusive) prison guards. His heart is as open and kind as his face. He brightened my day.

I thank the Playa Residency for two extraordinary weeks of focus and for reigniting my love of monotasking. Also for the sunrises. To Jody Swanson at Cloud & Leaf Books, profound appreciation for the house that has become my (our) writing retreat. To Scott Landfield at Tsunami Books, deep thanks for helping to provision the writers' group with books—and for your never-say-die love of writers. To Marty Brown at Oregon State University Press, profound thanks from sixty enthusiastic OSP readers for making possible the donation of *Stubborn Twig*.

And also: to Sarah Blondin, whom I have never met, for speaking the truth in my ear; to Alex Kotlowitz and Ted Conover, for naming it, practicing it, living it (the journalism of empathy); to the crew at Food for Lane County's Dining Room, especially Angie Godlasky, Josie McCarthy, Jesse Stafford, and Rene Speer, for modeling generosity of spirit, inclusion, and kindness; to Holly Lorincz, for long walks, longer talks, and understanding the joys and terrors of the work; to Keetje Kuipers, for bourbon, chocolate, and writerly camaraderie; to Kim Sheehan, for loyalty, support, encouragement, Americanos, and the ever-lasting warmth of true friendship.

I thank agent extraordinaire David Black for always believing and Jenny Herrera for her tireless (and I do mean tireless) efforts on the behalf of this book. I can hardly express the depth of my gratitude, Jenny. At Red Lightning, I thank my editor, Ashley Runyon, for her enthusiasm and support. I thank Darja Malcolm-Clarke, David Hulsey, and Michelle Sybert for their efforts on behalf of the book. At Amnet, I thank Leigh McLennon, Carol McGillivray, and Carmen Nickisch for their precision and care. It may not take a village, but it did take all of you.

I thank Trevor Walraven for showing me, the guys, and the "system" what is possible. I thank, with heart and soul, the men of the Lifers' Club writers' group, to whom this book is dedicated. You let me into your world. You trusted me. You educated me. You changed me.

And to my family: Liza Burns, for donating her design talents to the State Street Project; Jackson Hager, for years of computer crisis interventions; Zane Hager, for opening my mind and heart to restorative justice; Lizzie Hager, for showing me that strength and forgiveness go hand in hand. And Tom, partner and coconspirator in all. Grazie mille.

Sources

MANY HAVE STUDIED INCARCERATION—SOCIOLOGISTS, psychologists, criminologists, public health researchers, legal scholars, historians—and their work informed mine. A few journalists have managed to penetrate the walls surrounding prisons, and their work inspired mine. The best sources on the lives of the incarcerated are the incarcerated themselves.

Aiello, Antonio, and Jackson Taylor. *Handbook for Writers in Prison*. New York: PEN American Center, 2010.

Casella, Jean, James Ridgeway, and Sarah Shourd, eds. *Hell Is a Very Small Place*. New York: New Press, 2016.

Colsher, Patricia, Robert Wallace, Paul Loeffelholz, and Marilyn Sales. "Health Status of Older Male Prisoners: A Comprehensive Study." *American Journal of Public Health* 82, no. 6 (June 1992): 881–84.

Conover, Ted. *Newjack: Guarding Sing Sing*. New York: Random House, 2000.

Dumont, Dora, Brad Brockman, Samuel Dickman, Nicole Alexander, and Josiah Rich. "Public Health and the Epidemic of Incarceration." *Annual Review Public Health* 33 (2012): 325–29.

Earley, Pete. *The Hot House: Life inside Leavenworth Prison*. New York: Bantam, 1992.

Evans, Jeff, ed. *Undoing Time: American Prisoners in Their Own Words*. Boston: Northeastern University Press, 2001.

Fuller, John. *A Day in Prison: An Insider's Guide to Life Behind Bars*. With Holly Lorincz. New York: Skyhorse, 2017.

Garbarino, James. *Listening to Killers: Lessons Learned from My 20 Years as a Psychological Expert Witness in Murder Cases*. Oakland, CA: University of California Press, 2015.

Gopnik, Adam. "The Caging of America." *New Yorker*, January 30, 2012.

Hassine, Victor. *Life without Parole: Living and Dying in Prison Today*. New York: Oxford University Press, 2011.

Horton, David M., and George R. Nielsen. *Walking George: The Life of George John Beto and the Rise of the Modern Texas Prison System*. Denton, TX: University of North Texas Press, 2005.

Irwin, John. *The Felon*. Englewood Cliffs, NJ: Prentice Hall, 1970.

———. *Lifers: Seeking Redemption in Prison*. New York: Routledge, 2009.

Jackson, George. *Soledad Brother: The Prison Letters of George Jackson*. New York: Bantam, 1970.

Kerman, Piper. *Orange Is the New Black: My Year in a Women's Prison*. New York: Spiegel and Grau, 2010.

Krisberg, Barry, Susan Marchionna, and Christopher Hartney. *American Corrections: Concepts and Controversies*. Thousand Oaks, CA: Sage, 2015.

Liem, Marieke. *After Life Imprisonment: Reentry in the Era of Mass Incarceration*. New York: New York University Press, 2016.

Lifers' Unlimited Club. *Wisdom within the Pen*. Unpublished manuscript, Oregon State Penitentiary, Salem, OR, 2009.

Lipton, Douglas, Robert Martinson, and Judith Wilks. *The Effectiveness of Correctional Treatment: A Survey of Treatment Evaluation Studies*. New York: Praeger, 1975.

Mailer, Norman. *The Executioner's Song*. Boston: Little, Brown and Company, 1979.

Martinson, Robert. "New Findings, New Views: A Note of Caution Regarding Sentencing Reform." *Hofstra Law Review* 7, no. 2 (Winter 1979): 243–58.

———. "What Works?—Questions and Answers about Prison Reform." *Public Interest* (Spring 1974): 22–54.

Masters, Jarvis Jay. *Finding Freedom: Writings from Death Row*. Junction City, CA: Padma, 1997.

McCullough, Michael. *Beyond Revenge: The Evolution of the Forgiveness Instinct*. San Francisco: Jossey-Bass, 2008.

Miller, Jerome G. "Criminology." *Washington Post*, April 23, 1989.

———. "The Debate on Rehabilitating Criminals: Is It True That Nothing Works?" *Washington Post*, March 1989.

Morris, Norval, and David J. Rothman. *Oxford History of the Prison*. New York: Oxford University Press, 1995.

Mumola, Christopher. "Medical Causes of Deaths in State Prisons 2001–2004." US Department of Justice, Bureau of Justice Statistics Data Brief, NCJ 216340, January 2007.

Olive, Mark E. "Narrative Works." *University of Missouri-Kansas City Law Review* 77, no. 4 (Summer 2009).

Porter, Lauren, Shawn Bushway, Hui-Shien Tsao, and Herbert Smith. "How the U.S. Prison Boom Has Changed the Age Distribution of the Prison Population." *Criminology* 54, no. 1 (2016): 1–26.

Reed, Austin. *The Life and the Adventures of a Haunted Convict*. New York: Random House, 2016.

Schnittker, Jason, and Andrea John. "Enduring Stigma: The Long-Term Effects of Incarceration on Health." *Journal of Health and Social Behavior* 48 (June 2007): 115–30.

Schnittker, Jason, and Michael Massoglia. "A Sociocognitive Approach to Studying the Effects of Incarceration." *Wisconsin Law Review* (2015): 349–79.

Schnittker, Jason, Michael Massoglia, and Christopher Uggen. "Out and Down: Incarceration and Psychiatric Disorders." *Journal of Health and Social Behavior* 53, no. 4 (December 2012): 448–64.

Sentencing Project. *Life Goes On: The Historic Rise in Life Sentences in America*. Washington, DC: Sentencing Project, 2013.

Smith, Caleb. *The Prison and the American Imagination*. New Haven: Yale University Press, 2009.

Wicker, Tom. *A Time to Die*. New York: Quadrangle, 1975.

Wildeman, Christopher. "Incarceration and Health." In *Emerging Trends in the Social and Behavioral Sciences*, edited by Robert A. Scott, Stephen Michael Kosslyn, and Marlis Buchmann. Hoboken, NJ: Wiley and Sons, 2015. https://doi.org/10.1002 /9781118900772.etrds0179.

Williams, Brie, Marc Stern, Jeff Mellow, Meredith Safer, and Robert Greifinger. "Aging in Correctional Custody: Setting a Policy Agenda for Older Prisoner Health Care." *American Journal of Public Health* 102, no. 8 (August 2012): 1475–81.

LAUREN KESSLER is an award-winning author and immersion reporter who combines lively narrative with deep research to explore subcultures in our midst, from the gritty world of a maximum-security prison to the grueling world of professional ballet; from the hidden world of Alzheimer's sufferers to the stormy seas of the mother-daughter relationship. She is author of ten works of narrative nonfiction. Her other work includes *Raising the Barre: Big Dreams, False Starts and My Midlife Quest to Dance The Nutcracker*; *Counterclockwise: My Year of Hypnosis, Hormones, Dark Chocolate, and Other Adventures in the World of Anti-Aging*; *My Teenage Werewolf: A Mother, a Daughter, a Journey through the Thicket of Adolescence*; Pacific Northwest Book Award winner *Dancing with Rose* (published in paperback as *Finding Life in the Land of Alzheimer's*); *Washington Post* bestseller *Clever Girl*; and *Los Angeles Times* bestseller *The Happy Bottom Riding Club*—which David Letterman, in fierce competition with Oprah, chose as the first (and only) book for the Dave Letterman Book Club. She is also author of Oregon Book Award winner *Stubborn Twig*, which was chosen as the book for all Oregon to read in honor of the state's 2009 sesquicentennial.

Her journalism has appeared in the *New York Times Magazine*, the *Los Angeles Times Magazine*, *O* magazine, salon.com, the *Utne Reader*, *The Nation*, newsweek.com, *Prevention*, *Ladies' Home Journal*, and elsewhere. Kessler lives with her family in western Oregon.

laurenkessler.com
laurenchronicles.com